WORKING ON
THE BEATRIX POTTER
JIGSAW

TWENTY YEARS OF RESEARCH AND DISCOVERY

GW00319918

BEATRIX POTTER STUDIES IX

Papers presented at
The Beatrix Potter Society Conference
Ambleside, England, July 2000

Edited by Enid Bassom, Rowena Knox, Farnell Parsons, Irene Whalley

TITLE-PAGE ILLUSTRATION
The badge of the Beatrix Potter Society

FRONT COVER ILLUSTRATION
Hill Top by Night (watercolour)
(Linder Bequest, cat. No. 445)

BACK COVER ILLUSTRATION
Fly Agaric (*Amanita muscaria*) (watercolour and bodycolour)
(National Trust)

Produced by Sue Coley

ISBN 1 869980 19 0
Printed by The Bath Press Limited

Contents

Acknowledgements for Illustrations

The Beatrix Potter Society is grateful to the following for permission to reproduce illustrations:

Armitt Library & Museum, pp. 71, 72, 73, 78, 80

Chris Beetles Gallery, pp. 31, 41

B.W. Donaldson, p.14

Brigadier J. Heelis, OBE, p. 21

A.S. Hobbs, p. 99

National Trust, pp. 63, 82, 85

New Yorker magazine, p. 53

Free Library of Philadelphia, p. 87

The Pierpont Morgan Library, New York (MA2009, pp. 2 - 3), p. 22

R. Rawnsley, p. 92

Frederick Warne: Hill Top by Night (front cover) © 1971; Fly Agaric (*Amanita muscaria*) (back cover) © 1987; Cinderella, © 1985, p. 32 (Linder Bequest, V & A Museum); Rabbit Postman, p. 32 (Linder Bequest, V & A Museum); Old Mr Bunny, p. 33 (Linder Bequest, V & A Museum); Boy on a Mouse, p. 35 (Linder Collection); Who stole the tarts? p.38 (Linder Collection); caricature of Mrs Potter, p.39 (Linder Bequest., V & A Museum); corner of the schoolroom, © 1955, p. 56 (Linder Collection); foxglove and periwinkle, © 1955, p. 57 (Linder Collection); Derwentwater (watercolour), p. 63 (National Trust); illustration for p. 57 of *The Tale of Benjamin Bunny*, p. 66 © 1904, 1987; illustration for p. 44 of *The Tale of Mr Tod*, p. 67 © 1912, 1987; Old Man of the Woods (*Strobilomyces floccopus*), p. 71 © 1987; Velvet Shank (*Agaricus velutipes*), p. 73 © 1992; *Lachnellula wilkommii*, p. 78; *Crepidotus mollis*, p. 80; Wray Castle Library (Linder Bequest, V & A Museum), © 1955, p. 89; Mrs Heelis judging sheep, p. 91; Beatrix Potter with Canon Rawnsley and son (R. Rawnsley), p. 92

Victoria & Albert Museum, pp. 32, 33, 38, 39, 89

J.I. Whalley, pp. 94, 97

The following are from the Beatrix Potter Society's Photo Bank: pp.13, 18, 25, 46, 52, 93

The Beatrix Potter watercolours from the Armitt Collection, first published in *A Victorian Naturalist* (Warne 1992) are reproduced by kind permission of the Armitt Trustees.

Introduction

IN 2000 THE BEATRIX POTTER SOCIETY celebrated the twentieth year since its founding in November 1980. The biennial International Study Conference held in July 2000 reflected this anniversary by asking speakers to concentrate where possible on the research and discoveries which had taken place over the last twenty years. Over those years much new material about Beatrix Potter has come to light, and many aspects of her life and work have received fresh and detailed study. This volume, the ninth in the series *Beatrix Potter Studies*, commences, appropriately enough, with an account of the founding of the Society, which from the start has concentrated on the serious side of Beatrix Potter's work, eschewing any tendency to improve its Membership numbers by indulging in a 'Peter Rabbit Fan Club' attitude (*Irene Whalley*).

Another article shows how recently discovered material has shed new light on previously little-known aspects of Beatrix's life (*Judy Taylor*). The years have also enabled even the known work to be reconsidered in more detail, or in the light of new discoveries, so that our appreciation of the artwork is now greatly heightened (*Anne Hobbs*). Betsy Bray and *Jane Morse* both describe the very early interest shown by Americans in the little books, and Beatrix's appreciation of this interest, which has led to an increasing awareness of her work throughout the USA today. The very significant studies which have been made in the last twenty years concerning Beatrix Potter's scientific work, and her intense interest in the natural world, are admirably covered in the articles by *Peter Hollindale* and *Roy Watling*, and reveal clearly for the first time what a scientist we have lost in Beatrix Potter the writer and artist. Finally, and most appropriately at the end of the volume, are two articles which concern her later life as Mrs William Heelis, farmer, sheep-breeder and conservationist. Both authors have National Trust connections, which again reflects one of Beatrix Potter's great interests, shown so practically in her large bequest of property to the Trust. While *Christopher Hanson-Smith* details the rise of Beatrix's interest in the Trust and its work, *Paul Farrington* continues the story to the present day, including the Beatrix Potter Society's support for the various conservation projects undertaken at the present time.

Truly, the last twenty years have seen much infilling of the jigsaw which is the life and work of Beatrix Potter, 1866 – 1943, and in all of this the Beatrix Potter Society has played an important part – not least in the production of the present volume.

Notes on the Contributors

Betsy Bray is the Director of the Cora J. Belden Library in Rocky Hill, Connecticut. Before that, she was Children's Librarian at the Windsor Public Library for fifteen years, during which she was the recipient of the Faith H. Hektoen Award for excellence in children's library services from the Connecticut Library Association. Betsy received her Masters of Library Science degree from St John's University in New York, and it was through a children's literature course that her interest in Beatrix Potter began. A Member of the Beatrix Potter Society for seventeen years, she was instrumental in organising two American Beatrix Potter Society Conferences at the Free Library of Philadelphia, held in 1992 and 1999. Betsy has presented many slide talk programmes about Beatrix Potter throughout the United States and England.

Paul Farrington is one of the National Trust Wardens responsible for looking after the Trust's Hawkshead and Claife Estate. He has worked for the Trust for eight years, five in Hawkshead as Warden and three years as Estate Team Supervisor in the Duddon and Eskdale valleys, carrying out the day-to-day estate maintenance and project work. Prior to working for the Trust, he was with the Yorkshire Dales National Park as a Field Assistant on the Three Peaks Upland Footpath Repair Project, and he also worked as a seasonal Field Assistant at Malham. He was educated at Manchester Polytechnic, where he gained a BSc Honours in Geography and Environmental Studies.

Christopher Hanson-Smith followed a number of different occupations, including service in the Army and with the Overseas Civil Service in Nigeria, until, as he has phrased it, he came to the comparative calm of the National Trust. When told at his interview that with the new job went a cottage once lived in by Beatrix Potter, he said 'Beatrix who?'. His ignorance was soon remedied as he started to help in the management of Hill Top and the Heelis estate. He and his wife brought up their four children in Near Sawrey, so he has a close link with the Lake District, although he now lives in Norfolk. He was an early Member of the Society, and was its Chairman from 1984 until 1990.

Anne Stevenson Hobbs (Mrs Michael Wright) is the Frederick Warne Curator of Children's Literature at the National Art Library, Victoria and Albert Museum, and responsible for the Leslie Linder Bequest of Beatrix Potter material and other collections. She is the author or co-author of a number of books and articles, among them (with Joyce Irene Whalley) *Beatrix Potter: the V&A Collection* (1985); with Judy Taylor and others *Beatrix Potter, 1866-1943: the Artist and her World* (1987); and, with others, *A Victorian Naturalist* (1992). She also edited *Beatrix Potter's Art: a selection of paintings and drawings* (1989), and recently compiled the catalogue of *The Linder Collection* (1996). Anne Hobbs read Modern Languages and Social Anthropology at Newnham College, Cambridge. An accomplished violinist and lapsed pianist, she is a founder-member of the Mantegazza String Quartet, now the Blackfriars Quartet.

Peter Hollindale was Reader in English and Educational Studies at the University of York from 1965 until his recent retirement. He specialised in children's literature and Elizabethan drama, and established one of the earliest undergraduate courses on children's literature in British universities. His other special interests include Anna Sewell and J.M. Barrie – and of course Beatrix Potter. Among his writings are *Choosing Books for Children* (1974) and *Signs of Childness in Children's Books* (1997). An amateur naturalist since boyhood, he is a long-standing member of both the Yorkshire and the North Wales Wildlife Trusts. In 1997 he gave the Society's annual Linder Memorial Lecture, and also spoke at the Eighth International Study Conference in 1998.

Jane Morse, whose husband was the poet Samuel French Morse, grew up in Bangor, Maine, and was introduced to Beatrix Potter by the children's librarian there, who carried on the Anne Carroll Moore tradition of reading *The Tailor of Gloucester* at Christmas. She has lived and taught in New England, Japan, and New Zealand. In Boston she was associated with *The Horn Book Magazine*, and in 1982 she edited a selection of letters written by Beatrix Potter to her American friends, *Beatrix Potter's Americans*. Jane Morse has been the Society's American Liaison Officer since 1987, and has taken part in all the Society's Conferences since the first one in 1984.

Judy Taylor was a publisher for thirty years with the Bodley Head in London, specialising in books for children. She is Chairman of the Beatrix Potter Society and is a Trustee of Volunteer Reading Help, an organisation which works with children in primary schools on a one-to-one basis. The author of a number of books on Beatrix Potter, she has also written the texts for eleven children's picture books. She has edited and annotated *Beatrix Potter's Letters* and *Letters to Children from Beatrix Potter,* and for the Beatrix Potter Society, edited *The Choyce Letters* and *Beatrix Potter's Farming Friendship,* a collection of the letters Beatrix

Potter sent to her shepherd Joseph Moscrop. She is co-author with Patrick Garland of the one-woman play, *Beatrix*.

Roy Watling graduated from Sheffield University with first class honours in Botany and went to Edinburgh to complete a PhD. He then joined the staff of the Royal Botanic Garden, Edinburgh, where he stayed until 1998, when he was Head of Mycology and Plant Pathology. For short spells he was Acting Regius Keeper and Director, and Assistant Regius Keeper. Roy Watling is a Fellow of the Royal Society of Edinburgh, which in 1999 awarded him the Patrick Neill medal for contributions to mycology – a medal only awarded thirty times since 1851. For his research and teaching in mycology, especially abroad and to amateurs, he received the MBE in 1997. Roy Watling is also a Fellow of the Linnean Society of London, the Institute of Biology, and British and American mycological societies.

Joyce Irene Whalley was for many years on the staff of the National Art Library, Victoria and Albert Museum, where she was responsible for Manuscripts and Rare Books. The Museum's collection of early children's books (part of the Rare Book section) was considerably augmented with the arrival of the Linder Bequest of Beatrix Potter material. Irene Whalley has been involved in exhibitions and books from both sides of her Museum work, namely illuminated manuscripts and western calligraphy on the one hand, and the art of the book, especially children's book illustration, on the other. Her professional involvement with Beatrix Potter began with the first national exhibition of Potter's work, at the V & A Museum in 1971, and led in due course to her co-founding the Beatrix Potter Society in 1980 with Anne Clarke, then in charge of the Linder Collection at the National Book League. Her books include *'Cobwebs to Catch Flies': illustrated books for the nursery and schoolroom, 1700-1900* (1974), *A History of Writing Implements and Accessories* (1975), *A History of Children's Book Illustration* (with Tessa Chester) (1988), and *The Pens Excellencie: calligraphy of western Europe and America* (1980). She has written various books and articles on Beatrix Potter, including *Beatrix Potter's Derwentwater* (1988, 1995), and is at present co-editor of the Beatrix Potter Society *Newsletter*.

Checking the Record:
The Beatrix Potter Society in Retrospect

JOYCE IRENE WHALLEY

TWENTY YEARS AGO a small group of people used to meet about once a month after work to consider the formation of a Beatrix Potter Society. Two of us, Anne Clarke of the National Book League, and I, then at the Victoria and Albert Museum, were both in charge of parts of Leslie Linder's collection of original Beatrix Potter material. Anne Emerson was the Children's Books Editor at Frederick Warne, Beatrix's publishers, who were still located in Bedford Square as when Beatrix used to visit them, and so Anne was much involved with the little books. Then there was Jack Ladevèze, who was the Linder family's executor, and later we were joined by Brian Sibley, whom Anne Emerson introduced to us as another interested person. None of us really knew how to start a society, though each of us had had experience of belonging to one – which is not the same thing!

I remember those evenings very well, and how it seemed that as soon as we had settled one point, someone would say 'But what about . . .' and there seemed to be so many hurdles to jump over before one could say 'Here is a Beatrix Potter Society'. Today everything looks so fixed and solid that it is hard to realise that once it was all so fluid. Of course, we never had to worry about a *name* for the Society – but what about a recognisable logo? The Mouse Reading seems so right now, but various alternatives were discussed first. Notepaper? Of course – but what colour and what sort of heading? – and so it went on. What really gave us form was Jack's idea that we should seek charitable status, and this he offered to do for us. In order to apply for this we first had to have a Constitution, and the formulation of this finally gave the new Society its firm foundation. Such facts are all rather boring, but they are the bricks of a solid building which, as we can see, has stood for twenty years, and which we hope will continue to survive. We had no money to start with, but

Frederick Warne kindly gave us £200 for the paper, photocopying, stamps and other necessities, and by November 1980 we were ready to place announcements in papers and libraries – our Chairman, Brian Sibley, was particularly good on the media side. By early in 1981 we were ready to launch ourselves in the USA and before long we had our Liaison Officer there to look after the interests of our American Members – and Jane Morse is still serving the Society in that capacity today.

Having formed a Society, what do you do with it? Well, ideally you bring the Members together by holding meetings – but our Membership was spread throughout the UK and overseas. So we started a *Newsletter* to keep people in touch, and to circulate information about books, exhibitions, and any other relevant activities. I think everyone will agree that the *Newsletter* is the most important aspect of the Society, binding together all those who share a common interest. I do not say this just because I am one of the current editors, for from the beginning the Society has been served by a succession of editors, all of whom have kept up a very high standard of content and presentation. As techniques have improved, so has the *Newsletter,* and what is better, more and more of our Members are contributing to it.

I personally came to Beatrix Potter as an art historian and as a writer on early children's books. Anne Clarke, my co-founder, was a librarian with literary interests. So those two aspects dominated the Society's early years. I think it was our first Study Conference in 1984 which really opened our eyes to the wider interests of our Members. Enid Bassom and I had rather anxiously organised this first Conference, by no means sure who would come to it – or, indeed if anyone would be interested. The support surprised us, especially that from the USA. Today it will probably surprise many people that we should have been so surprised! Among the first participants from the States we found puppeteers of considerable renown and collectors with a great deal of knowledge of their chosen subject. As we travelled around the Lake District on planning tours for the first and subsequent Conferences, we began to learn more about Beatrix Potter's farming interests, and then about her holidays in various parts of the country. So gradually the scope of the Society broadened to take account of these factors, and at the same time our American Membership began to organise its own Conferences, thus opening up new sources of information – something which had been set in motion by Jane Morse's edition of Beatrix's letters to her American friends.

The Society has never been static, but has continually evolved and developed over the years. What surprises me is how much of the foundation laid all that time ago has proved so firm, and has remained the basis for the work of the

Committee and for the organisation of the Society to this day. We may now have computers, and communicate by e-mail, but, thank goodness, the friendly informality among Members remains an outstanding feature of the Society.

Certainly we must never let ourselves get too formalised or too remote. Beatrix Potter would have hated that. I smile to myself sometimes, when today we wear white gloves to handle original Potter drawings or watercolours, and then think back to the 1970s, just before the Society began. I remember going to the National Trust in Ambleside with a colleague to look at Potter material for an exhibition at the Victoria and Albert Museum. We were shown into a room where three black metal boxes had been placed on the floor, and we were more or less invited to dive in. We did! A little later, at Hill Top, when research-ing for our book *Beatrix Potter's Derwentwater,* we were shown drawers and cupboards in a rather chilly and damp upper room in the house (it was early spring!), and invited to browse through the contents to find what might be of interest. Later, when we wanted to photograph some items, a kitchen chair was carried out into the garden for us, on which the items were placed, because the light was better for photography out there! I can imagine that any curator today would be horrified if it happened now – and, I hasten to assure you, so would the National Trust itself these days! But it is a measure of how things have changed since the Society was first discussed, and no doubt we can expect to see more changes in the future. Perhaps it will even come about that Beatrix's orig-inal watercolours will never be shown at all, because their mechanical repro-duction will look better than what Beatrix actually drew or painted! In some ways that has already happened. When the modern firm of Frederick Warne (part of Penguin Books) undertook in the 1980s the re-origination of all Beatrix Potter's illustrations for the little books, it became clear that in some cases we were already seeing the published pictures far closer to her original paintings than she herself ever did, simply because of improved techniques of colour reproduction.

So far in looking back over the Society's record, I have only considered how it came about, and the development of its *Newsletter*. But, somewhat to its own surprise, the Society also became a publisher and a collector. Coming from the academic world, I had always had it impressed on me that knowledge was for sharing – something also well-known to teachers and librarians. So after the dust of the first Conference had settled, we set about publishing the talks in order that they might be shared with the rest of the Membership. Our first efforts were a little tentative, as those of you who have *Beatrix Potter Studies I* will know. The content was all right, since we had a good selection of speakers, but the format was wrong, and brown ink is not easy to read either. We learnt as we went along, and subsequent *Studies* can, I think, stand up with the best. Our Treasurer at the time was Enid Bassom and she felt very strongly that our publications should be as cheap as was consistent with quality, so that Members could buy them at almost cost price, and that policy still holds good today. But it does have a down-side. We should like to sell our publications more widely, but book-sellers expect large discounts, which you cannot give if you are already selling at near cost price. So that although our sales are thereby limited, at least you can be sure that when you buy a Society publication you are getting what may well prove to be a rare collectors' item in the future!

The very first object which the Society bought in its role as a collector was the rescue purchase of a little volume written out and bound by Leslie Linder. This was published by the Society as *Peter Rabbit's Other Tale* (usually known to the Committee as PROT!) and it has proved to be our most popular publication. The manuscript contained Canon Rawnsley's awful verse form of Beatrix's *The Tale of Peter Rabbit,* which he wrote in the hope that it would prove more accept-able to publishers than the original. I can still remember how the Members pre-sent at one of our meetings squirmed with pleasurable horror – or do I mean horrible pleasure? – when Judy Taylor read it all through to us, beginning with:

There were four little bunnies, no bunnies were sweeter
Mopsy and Cotton-tail, Flopsy and Peter.
They lived in a sandbank as here you may see
At the foot of a fir, a magnificent tree.

This gem of literature, you will be pleased to know, is safely housed in the Victoria and Albert Museum, and it is an interesting sidelight on what might have been – but for the good sense of Frederick Warne and Beatrix herself! The Society's version of it is now in its third printing.

But not all our purchases have been suitable for publication, any more than our publications have always been linked to our purchases. We have been delighted to acquire a Peter Rabbit teaset from its original owner, knowing that Beatrix Potter concerned herself personally over its production, and likewise the *Peter Rabbit Race-Game,* with which she was also involved. We were also very pleased when Brigadier John Heelis offered us a box of imitation food, just like that depicted in *The Tale of Two Bad Mice.*

One of our most poignant purchases, which did become a publication, was the holiday diary kept by Beatrix Potter soon after she got engaged to Norman Warne. Her demanding parents had immediately carried her off to North Wales, and it was during their time there that Norman died. Unlike her *Journal,* the diary was written in long-hand. Maybe she could no longer write her code

12

The Peter Rabbit teaset made by the firm of Grimwade in 1922, with Beatrix Potter's approval. Purchased by the Society from the original owner in 1991

with fluency by then, but my personal opinion is that she kept it that way so that Norman could eventually read how she spent her days in Wales – except, of course, that the daily record stops dead when she got the devastating news of his sudden death. The rest was subsequently written up in retrospect. This *Holiday Diary* has been admirably edited by Judy Taylor.

Next to the *Journal,* the letters give us the best insight into Beatrix's life, and here the Society has been well-served by its Members Jane Morse and Judy Taylor. How much more we now know about Beatrix's life, and about her thoughts on everything from art to animals and from furniture to farming, thanks to the work of those two. But I know Judy has many more copies of letters than have been printed to date, and I am sure that there are more in America than have so far appeared – so, American Members, please take note!

Indeed, I think there is quite a bit of work for our American Members to do. A lot of Beatrix Potter material has made its way across the pond in recent years, and we need to know more about the collections there. It has been very exciting to hear of the success of the Conferences held at Santa Barbara, Philadelphia and elsewhere – and to learn of other, more modest but equally keen meetings, as when Members from Indiana have all got together. What a unifying instrument the little books have become! At our Conferences in the Lake District we have had speakers from the United States, France and Japan, and participants from Holland, Denmark, Japan and Russia, while theses have been presented by French, Canadian and Italian students. Our Society exists to promote the work of Beatrix Potter in all its aspects and this promotion is where every Member can play a part.

But in this twenty-first century we do need to ask ourselves 'where do we want to go from here?' Having followed the fortunes of the Society from its inception, I naturally have strong feelings on what I should like for the future. I think that in publishing works and rescuing objects we have done quite a lot to justify the aims proclaimed in our Constitution. But to my mind the best thing we have done – and are still doing – is the *Reading Beatrix Potter* project. For us older people, reading has always been taken for granted, as part of life. This is no longer so. Every young child today has so many alternative calls on his or her attention, that reading – which requires some effort – can fall by the way-side, and the little books could fade away. But the response of children in both the United Kingdom and the United States has amply proved the value of the work done by our band of volunteer Readers in introducing children to the joy of books.

I should also like to see the continued publication of material relating to Beatrix Potter. At some time a brave soul will have to tackle a revision of her coded *Journal*. Leslie Linder provided us with an invaluable tool and source-book, but his work is nearly forty years old now, and much new light could be thrown on the text, as the recent series in the *Newsletter* of *Footnotes to the Journal* has shown. And there were, inevitably, some inaccurate transcriptions. So there's another job for an aspiring scholar!

The joy of reading Beatrix Potter: Clemmie Welsh Donaldson holds one of the large-size books used for group reading

14

Duchess in Sawrey: an unused drawing for *The Tale of the Pie and the Patty-Pan*, purchased by the Society at a New York auction, and used for a set of Notelets

We have also learnt much in recent years about Mrs Heelis, and her life in the Lake District. This was the time when she was at her happiest, and when she involved herself deeply in new commitments. The Society has been very aware of this aspect of her life, and we know too that many Members share Beatrix's concern for the conservation of the natural world – this is amply proved by the way donations are so generously given towards the various projects associated with footpaths, stone walls, the preservation of old buildings and other matters dear to Beatrix herself.

So there is no shortage of ideas for the future work of the Society. Based on a firm foundation, and with a willingness to share experiences and work together, the future looks good. BUT, and it is a big BUT – in these days when money talks so often and so loudly, the Society does need people to come forward and help, as we older ones retire – people ready to give up their time, which is far more valuable than money. It was the voluntary spirit which built up the Society, and which has kept it going, as the Committee and Conference Organisers on both sides of the Atlantic agree. I am a survivor. I have seen Chairmen come and go, and likewise a variety of Office Holders and humble Committee Members. They have all played their part in bringing the Society to its present position, and I would like to pay tribute to those who, over the last twenty years, have served it so well and then gone their ways. The Society has survived this far because of all those who in the past were there when they were most wanted and who gave so generously of their time. We need more like them to ensure the Society's continued well-being over the next twenty years – and I am sure we shall find them, since there is too much goodwill around to allow the Society to fade away through lack of active support.

Keeping the Pieces Together: the Beatrix Potter Jigsaw in the United Kingdom

JUDY TAYLOR

I FIND THAT I have been presented with a mammoth task – to sum up in a short space 'the research and discoveries relating to Beatrix Potter's life that have taken place in the UK since the founding of the Society'. And what that really means is surveying everything that has come to light in the last twenty years. A mammoth task indeed and one that I cannot hope to achieve. What I shall attempt to do, however, is to highlight some of the most interesting discoveries of the last twenty years.

And here I should like to pay a special tribute to the Society's Vice-President, Dr Mary Noble. Mary has been a Society Member since the very early days, but even before then she had embarked upon the Potter trail. She has been responsible for supplying so many pieces of the Potter jigsaw, from 'funguses' to photographs, from paintings to gravestones. Her extraordinary story really begins before the Society was formed, for it was in the early 1970s that this eminent mycologist was researching the history of mycology - the study of fungi - in Scotland. Her own account of how she came upon Beatrix Potter's involvement in the matter is well documented in that most handsome publication *A Victorian Naturalist* and I quote from the Personal Preface to her section 'Beatrix Potter and Charles McIntosh, Naturalists':

> [I] was particularly interested in the life and works of Charles McIntosh (1839-1922), known as the Perthshire Naturalist . . .. When he died, a book to commemorate him was compiled by Henry Coates. After publication the relevant papers were returned to Charles McIntosh's niece, Miss E.M. MacIntosh . . . who kept the parcel unopened for fifty years until I asked her for more information about her uncle. . . . I found many extremely interesting papers . . . but I was astonished to find also letters from the Potter family, three from Mr Rupert Potter and twelve from his daughter Beatrix. These were all about what she called 'funguses', lichens and even mosses.

Mary Noble had made an important discovery which was to change our knowledge of one crucial period in Beatrix's life. In the first edition of her biography *The Tale of Beatrix Potter*, published in 1946, Margaret Lane wrote (with that wonderful use of language which was her trademark):

> If there were a mystery anywhere in this simplest and most innocent of lives, it would be in the silence and blankness stretched like a skin over the decade from [Beatrix's] seventeenth to her twenty-seventh year. Almost nothing is known about it, for the apparently sufficient reason that there is nothing to know. . . [except that] at some point in it she took up, and at another abandoned, the study of fungus.

What Margaret Lane did not know was that Beatrix's coded *Journal*, full of references to her fungi discoveries and her recording of them, and to her encounters with the authorities at Kew and the Linnean Society, was lying ignored in a drawer in Castle Cottage – and that the loosely gathered pages would remain there for another six years, and then be unseen for another fourteen years while they were in the care of Leslie Linder.

Mary Noble's next piece of research was to seek out Beatrix's fungi watercolours - in the Perth Museum and Gallery, in the Armitt Library in Ambleside, and in the Victoria and Albert Museum in London - and then either to identify them or to confirm their given names. This, incidentally, appears to me to be a continuing and never-ending task, as botanists and mycologists seem to be constantly changing all the names for some reason or another, something I fail to understand and I believe is a plot to force publishers to issue new editions of identification books, or to confuse the amateur. Mary, however, being the professional that she is, is able to keep up with it all.

Roy Watling's article deals with Beatrix's 'funguses', so I will not dwell much longer on them myself. However, I do have one more Potter fungus discovery story to tell about Mary, and this comes under the heading of discovery rather than research. During the Society's Second Conference, in 1986, a number of us were having lunch in the Tower Bank Arms in Near Sawrey when the then proprietor approached the group carrying a dark and dusty picture which he said had been hanging on the wall in one of the back rooms. Showing it to the assembled company, he said, 'She did that, you know, Beatrix Potter'. At once Mary identified the picture as one of Beatrix's previously unseen fungus paintings, *Amanita muscaria* or Fly Agaric (see back cover). Those of you who have read Willow Taylor's book, *Through the Pages of my Life,* will know that the Tower Bank Arms has been owned since 1976 by the National Trust, so this most beautiful picture is now part of their valued Potter Archives – and it no longer hangs on the wall of their pub.

17

The much-valued Mary Noble features once again in the next piece of the jig-saw, this time concerning Beatrix Potter's brother, Bertram. In January 1982 the journalist Liz Taylor reported in the Society's *Newsletter* No.4 how, a year or so before, she had stumbled across the information that Bertram Potter had once lived and farmed in her own village of Ancrum in the Scottish Borders, and this started her off on the Bertram trail. She was soon to discover that Bertram had indeed farmed at a house called Ashyburn in Ancrum for many years and that his grave was said to be in the village churchyard. It took Liz a long time to find the grave, but find it she did, buried under the ivy and general overgrowth of many years, and she then, 'Danced for joy along the rain soaked path, for I felt like Stanley meeting Dr Livingstone in Darkest Africa'.

I first came across Liz Taylor's story the year before she wrote that for the *Newsletter*, when I was starting the research for my book *Beatrix Potter: Artist, Storyteller and Countrywoman*. It was in an article entitled 'The Tale of Bertram Potter' published in the May 1981 issue of *Woman's Realm*, a copy of which had been sent by a Potter enthusiast to Anne Hobbs for the Victoria and Albert Museum Collection. Mary Noble's encounter with Liz Taylor, however, was typical of the sort of coincidence that continually happens to the researcher. Mary had gone to Hawick, which is not far from Ancrum, as she was also on the Bertram Potter trail. One of her first calls was to the Hawick Museum where she met Liz Taylor's daughter who just happened to be working there. Of course, the magic words 'Beatrix Potter' resulted in a meeting between the two enthusiasts, and when she heard about Liz Taylor's discovery of Bertram's grave, Mary launched into yet another campaign.

When Beatrix's brother Walter Bertram Potter died in 1918, she wrote in a letter to Canon Rawnsley, 'He is buried like the Grasmere folks in the bend of a stream – a flow-ery graveyard, with a ruined ivy-grown church and graves of the covenanters on the banks of Ale Water'. Now, some sixty-five years later, as Liz Taylor had discov-ered, the graveyard was so overgrown that it was

Dr Mary Noble, with the Ancrum graveyard and Bertram Potter's burial place in the background

18

almost impenetrable, but Mary resolved that Bertram's grave should be restored to a condition of which the Beatrix Potter Society could be proud.

It appears that in Scotland the local council is responsible for the state of all graves for a full hundred years after they have been established, and Mary, who of course was aware of this particular bye-law, started what she calls her 'bullying' of the Ancrum council to face up to their responsibilities. Knowing Mary as well as we do, it was *not* altogether surprising that within a reasonably short time Bertram's grave had been restored to its former glory, the whole graveyard had been cleared and the grass neatly mown. In 1986, during the Post- Conference Tour to Scotland, Society Members made their first visit to the grave and there they proudly saw the brightly shining, newly re-gilded lettering, 'In memory of Walter Bertram Potter of Ashyburn, Ancrum, the Beloved husband of Mary Potter, Born 14th March 1872, Died 22nd June 1918. Peace Perfect Peace'.

It was an American Member of the Society who was responsible for the next important piece of research, a book called *Beatrix Potter's Americans: Selected Letters*, published by The Horn Book in Boston in 1982. Jane Crowell Morse had brought together one hundred and sixty-four of the letters from Beatrix Potter to a dozen or so of the Americans who visited her in Sawrey during the last twenty years of her life: librarians, publishers, editors, young fans and admirers from New England. Beatrix liked the open approach of Americans, for, as Jane Morse says in her introduction, 'They were neither curiosity-seekers nor idle trippers, but candid, friendly, spontaneous visitors from across the Atlantic with whom she felt relaxed and able to share common interests'. The publication of *Beatrix Potter's Americans* revealed a valuable and entirely new aspect of Beatrix Potter's life, and the book gave a number of its readers the impetus and inspiration to find out even more.

Irene Whalley has written in her article about the Society's purchase in 1988 of Leslie Linder's transcription of Hardwicke Rawnsley's rhyming version of *The Tale of Peter Rabbit* - published the following year as *Peter Rabbit's Other Tale*, so I will not repeat the story, but I cannot resist reminding you of the awfulness of the rhyme. You will recognise what stage the tale has reached when you hear this:

> At last Peter sat on a/ door step to rest
> With a stitch in his side/ and dark fear in his breast
> He shook with the cold/ had a spasm of cramp
> For where Peter had hid/ was decidedly damp.

Or maybe you remember this verse? Thankfully it is an episode that does not appear in Beatrix Potter's version:

There are bucks among men/ there are bucks among rabbits
Much more than we think/ we have all the same habits
And here is a portrait/ without any joke
Of a buck of a rabbit / enjoying a smoke.

The Society's publications programme reflects much of its Members' researches and discoveries. The publication in 1993 of *A Beatrix Potter Photograph Album*, to mark the fiftieth year since Beatrix Potter's death, enabled everyone to see for the first time the images from Rupert Potter's old glass photographic plates that had been given to the Society in its earliest days by Leslie Linder's executor, Jack Ladevèze. When developing and printing his work, Rupert Potter was meticulous in pencilling on to the back of each photograph the date, the place and frequently the exposure, but with the glass negatives this was not possible. For our captions, therefore, we had to rely on the expert knowledge of those people who had already done a good deal of Potter research - all of them, not unexpectedly, Members of the Society. As no one had seen photographs of Beatrix at such an early age before and as there were no references to which we could turn, the captions to some photographs had by necessity to be somewhat vague, i.e. 'Beatrix at the age of five[?], probably in London'.

Another photograph we captioned 'Beatrix at Dalguise', which is not a lot more informative, but we knew that the photograph had been taken at Dalguise because the chair, the coat and the step in the background were all identifiable from other, marked, photographs. What we had no clue to was the date, so we did not even try to suggest Beatrix's age.

I find myself increasingly in the position of 'one who is supposed to know', and that is a considerable responsibility; as time goes on, I become more hesitant. Take the famous wedding photograph. I related in *Newsletter* No. 71 how I came to be misled about this, but I will tell the story again, as it is such a good example of how easy it is to jump to a conclusion. One of the great dangers in research is assuming something which then all too quickly becomes part of the accepted story.

For years everyone has called this 'The Wedding Picture', and for years we have all marvelled at Beatrix's apparent disdain of fashion on that special day, and at Willie Heelis for allowing her to stand while he so comfortably occupied the only seat. We have also accepted without question that the date written on the only available print, 14 October 1913, *(not* in Rupert Potter's hand I hasten to emphasise) was the date of Beatrix's wedding, for it is, after all, the date given for the wedding by both Margaret Lane and Leslie Linder in their respective books and, I regret to report, cravenly followed by me in the first five editions of my own book, *Artist, Storyteller and Countrywoman*.

The so-called 'wedding picture'

It was not until comparatively recently, when for some other purpose altogether I had obtained a facsimile copy of Beatrix and Willie's wedding certificate, that I saw the wedding had in fact taken place on the following day, 15 October 1913. Soon afterwards I was shown, for the first time, Rupert Potter's original print of the photograph, and there on the back, in his unmistakable writing, was confirmation that the date on which he had taken the photograph was 14 October 1913, the day *before* the wedding. So whoever had originally copied the photograph had been quite correct about the date it was taken but incorrect in calling it 'The Wedding Picture'. Being in the position of a discoverer and a researcher can have its dangers.

While I am on the subject of Rupert Potter photography, I am delighted to be able to tell you about a few of the nearly two hundred of his photographs from the Doris Frohnsdorff Collection, which the Society recently purchased in New York. All the photographs are of considerable interest from the research point of view, giving us new dates and confirming others, and adding to the list of places for Potter holidays and visits. And many of the photographs are outstandingly beautiful. There is one of a cluster of farm buildings in Watendlath in the Lake District, photographed in September 1885, just one hundred and fifteen years ago, and another of a Lake District farm at Wythburn in September 1897. Harvesting in Thirlmere was photographed the following year, in July

21

1898, and in a group of people to the top left-hand of the picture there is a horse and carriage standing in the road behind the wall, with a boy perched up at the back, and a young woman in white sitting behind the coachman. That summer the whole Potter family were spending their holiday at Lingholm . . . . Then there are also Rupert Potter's London photographs. Among the many things that we learn from them is that he visited the London Zoo at least six times in the early summer of 1901 - on 23, 24, 26 April, 7 June, 15 June and 11 July, photographing two delightful hippopotamuses on 11 July and a giraffe on 7 June. We know from her letters that Beatrix was not with her father on these particular occasions, although we do know she was a regular visitor to the Zoological Gardens and from a letter which she wrote to Noel Moore in 1895, that she particularly liked the giraffes:

> March 8 - I went to the zoo on Wednesday & saw the new giraffe. It is a young one, very pretty, and the keeper says it will grow a good deal taller. I saw the box that it came in, the keeper says that it had quite a stiff neck because the box was not large enough. They brought it by train from Southampton and they could not have a larger box because of getting through the tunnels.

We also know from her letters that Beatrix was at the Zoo in March 1903 to

A page from Beatrix's letter to Noel Moore about her vist to the Zoological Gardens in 1895

22

draw an owl for the new endpaper for the Warne edition of *The Tailor of Gloucester;* that she was there on 14 April 1905 to draw a magpie for *The Tale of the Pie and the Patty-Pan;* again on 10 October 1912 when she took her dairy maid there for a treat; and in March 1919 to draw the bear for *The Tale of Timmy Tiptoes.*

For all students of the Potter story, one of the most important aspects of our purchase of these photographs is that it has enabled us to secure at least a few examples of Rupert Potter's remarkable chronicle of London in the 1880s and 1890s. With the strange and tragic disappearance in 1992 of over 1,000 of his photographs from the Civic Trust collection it was feared that perhaps this valuable record might have been lost for ever.

Over the years I have spoken and written a number of times about the important place Beatrix Potter's own writing takes, whether it be in her letters or in her diary, in helping us to work on the Potter jigsaw, and here I should like to give credit to the Society's Committee in encouraging the publication of some of these finds, thus fulfilling Item 2 of The Beatrix Potter Society Constitution, which states:

> The Society shall seek to educate the public in and promote research into the life and works of Beatrix Potter by all the charitable ways that the Society believes would have met with her approval and the Society shall publish the results of the research; and in furtherance of these objects, but not further or otherwise, the Society will have the following powers:
>
> (a) to afford a means of communication for the exchange of ideas between scholars and others who have a mutual interest in the life and works of Beatrix Potter;
>
> (b) to hold meetings where knowledge and opinion about the life and works of Beatrix Potter can be communicated, shared and discussed;
>
> (c) to arrange visits to places of interest connected with the life and works of Beatrix Potter;
>
> (d) at suitable times to sponsor and support special charitable projects relating to the life and works of Beatrix Potter;
>
> (e) to produce or assist in the production of publications promoting these objects;
>
> (f) when funds permit, to purchase at auction or on any other occasion items by or relating to Beatrix Potter;
>
> (g) to do all lawful things necessary to advance the objects.

Not a bad aim, is it? The Conference in July 2000 fulfilled (a) 'means of communication and exchange of ideas', (b) 'a meeting where knowledge and opinion is communicated, shared and discussed' and (c) 'visits to places connected with etc'. Your Committee makes sure that the Society does the rest - (d) 'sponsor and support charitable projects', (e) 'produce and assist in the production of publications', (f) 'purchase at auction', and (g) 'do all lawful things necessary to advance the objects'.

However, none of these things would be possible without the co-operation of all the Members of the Society and without their generous donations. It is their support that enables us to do our discovery and research. Without the donations we would not have been able to buy the manuscript of *A Holiday Diary* at auction in 1994 and to publish it in 1996, to publish *The Choyce Letters* in 1994 and *The Moscrop Letters* in 1998, or to bring Willow Taylor's memoirs, *Through the Pages of My Life,* into print this year.

But contributions from Members to the Society's researches and discoveries do not come only in financial form, and this is where I should like to make another particular and personal thank you. It is to Elaine Jacobsen, who has spent a great deal of her time in the last few years working on a number of indexes. In 1994 Elaine compiled (and indeed then printed for Members) an index to the first fifty issues of the *Newsletter*. She followed that in 1996 with the index to *Newsletters 51-60*. In 1998 she indexed the first six volumes of *Beatrix Potter Studies,* the records of all our Conference talks, and in 1999 she finished a very full index for the 1989 revised edition of the *Journal*. As someone who refers to one or the other (if not all) of these publications practically every week of my life, Elaine's indexes have proved to be extremely valuable tools and a very real contribution to the study of the Potter story.

I am sometimes asked what is the point of all this research into the life of Beatrix Potter? Can there possibly be anything more to discover? And why do we bother to do it, anyway? For me, it is an intriguing challenge, as I suspect it is for all of us involved in the field - and I really love the fun of the chase. I also know that perhaps the main consequence of all the work that has been done over the past twenty years is that it has completely changed our concept of Beatrix Potter.

For nearly twenty years Margaret Lane's *The Tale of Beatrix Potter* was the only source of information about her. I still remember well the extraordinary impact that book had on the world, when for the first time we read the remarkable story of our favourite picture-book creator who became a farmer. However, as so often happens to all those who were first in a particular field, subsequent research and discoveries have revealed that Margaret Lane was not entirely correct in some of her interpretations and assumptions. For instance, her description of 'the barred third-floor windows' of No 2 Bolton Gardens behind which Beatrix was 'stationed day after day' was cited by Lane as proof that the

The young Beatrix Potter, photographed by her father, date and place unknown. Printed from a glass negative in the Society's collection

young girl was imprisoned there by her cruel parents, when in reality every window of every child's nursery in houses of that size had barred windows, for the very practical reason that they were intended to stop children falling out.

It was Margaret Lane who started the myth that Beatrix did not get on at all well with her father, and it was not until the publication in 1966 of the *Journal* that we were able to read for ourselves Beatrix's numerous affectionate accounts of her relationship with her father – about the time he took her to the art shop to buy her first box of paints, or when they discussed politics and painting together, and of the many times father and daughter drove out together in Scotland, in Cornwall and in the Lake District, sharing their love of photography and the beauty of the landscape.

There is in my Potter letters file an early letter from Rupert to his seven year-old daughter which reveals his deep affection for her:

Dalguise House, Dunkeld, North Britain [which is what some people then called Scotland]. Monday March 2 1874.
My dear B, I have sent a letter to Mamma but I know you will like to have one from me . . .. I have given the chestnuts to Cleghorn to sow. I have seen three young trees – they are very strong. The white cat from the stables lives in the house and has kept away the rats and mice very well all winter. There are some snowdrops on the lawn but the trees are all bare and no bunnies are to be seen. McIntosh got a fine salmon on Saturday and sent it to Mr Tom Potter. Now if you read this letter I shall be very glad and I am dear B
Your affectionate Papa.

From what we have discovered through our research we now look at Beatrix Potter in quite a different way from how we saw her twenty years ago. As letters have come to light they have opened up her world to us, shown her in her role as farmer, gardener, even furniture collector, and sometimes the discovery of a letter offers yet another aspect of her fascinating character. I am going to end with some more extracts from some of the many as-yet-unpublished letters from the file, which I think will illustrate what I mean.

This is Beatrix writing to Norman Warne's sister, Millie, in April 1916, showing her practical approach to business when she was beginning to have suspicions that all was not well at Warne:

> It seems a long time since I heard any news of you, or Bedford Street . . . I hope they are doing better, or less anxiously at all events . . .. I am not hard up, and have no intention of behaving unkindly by pressing them - of which the rascals are probably aware! I do sometimes wonder whether they presume a little in that knowledge, or whether things are so difficult as they seem. I have never yet got accounts for Pigling Bland, let alone any of that season's money . . .. I think I shall probably ask to have a fresh agreement about the books; they certainly have not been able to keep to the agreement on their side; and I don't like the indefinite wording of the papers. If anything happened to any of us – I mean death which comes to all mankind - there would be such a terrible muddle for somebody to unravel. I am only saying this to you that you may understand I am not doing anything in unkindness of spirit, if you hear presently your brothers saying that I insist on having something settled - [it is] about the account keeping rather than the money.

And here is Beatrix the art critic, teacher and observer of nature, writing to the painter, Delmar Banner, in October 1937, from whom she had just bought a painting:

> Perhaps sometime if you are at a loose end in Sussex exile you might consider studying trees, having mastered the form of clouds. You don't care to choose landscape low enough to require much appreciation but it is useful to understand them. And incredible how badly many professional woodland landscape painters don't. I mean they have never considered how the branches grow from a tree trunk. For instance the ash, 'igdrasil', the tree of heaven. Every year a new shoot [and] if you study an ash you will see every branch from the main trunk, or the stem of the young sapling, has come out in curves; and curved on and on with the weight of foliage. Other species in contrast grow upward. We can tell every tree in winter without reference to foliage by its mode of growth. So study them some spare moments, Mr Banner; they will repay – they are in the right place as beautiful as rocks. They have a nobility of growth which is usually entirely over looked.

And now Beatrix the down-to-earth employer - and, incidentally, the feminist aware of her position in society - from a letter to Augusta Burn in January 1916, when things were starting to become difficult on the farms in the First World War:

> I have had a perplexing time about the recruiting, but in the end my ploughman is to stay. . .. I was strong that he ought to remain till I could sow down the arable land; but on the whole I think he is more properly exempt [from the

army] than many . . .. For myself (always provided the land got sown down) - I was indifferent; as I could work it as a grass farm; I had rather looked forward to employing women - no that is unkind to the ploughboy. I think there will have to be more [women] on the land in future - but in my opinion they will be ladies - the sham 'lidies' turned out by the board schools are so despicably afraid of dirtying their hands.

And finally, the Beatrix who knew how to write to children. This is from a letter written in October 1916 to seven year-old Nancy Nicholson, William Heelis's niece, who had recently been to stay:

> I have a lot to tell you. You left a small blackboard out of your lesson box, and Judy [the cat] has begun a school. Miny went to get the kittens out of Uncle Willie's work shop, and she said there was an animule with them. It was rather dark in the shop. It was Mrs Tiggywinkle's [sic] youngest child called Pricklepin. It has rather a large head and is backward; it has not written any more words on the board yet, but Judy is teaching it to sing. I do not know how long it has been at school, perhaps an inch! It is quite friends with the kittens, when I brought them into the kitchen, they all drank milk out of one saucer . . .. It has a little black nose and very small eyes just like old Tiggywinkle [sic]. I should like to keep it, but I am afraid it might bite the rabbits . . .. Uncle Willie and I send best love to you all.
> Your affectionate Auntie Beatrix.

That Beatrix herself was intrigued by research is shown by this extract from a letter she sent to her cousin, Edith Gaddum, in December 1921: 'At first I was bored but we have worked out such ramifications of the family tree that I have become interested'. Sadly, no record of their discoveries has yet been found but who knows what will come to light tomorrow?

Context and Content: Working on Beatrix Potter's Art

ANNE STEVENSON HOBBS

A T THE FIRST Study Conference in 1984, I described 'Beatrix Potter collections in the British Isles', concentrating on her art and manuscripts rather than on printed books. Re-reading that paper brings home to me how much progress has since been made. Firstly, public collections are better organised, and we know more about private collections. Secondly, our approach has changed and developed. Thirdly, a lot of new material has come to light.

Our knowledge of Beatrix Potter's art is continually increasing: what she created, and where it is now; how she worked, who influenced her art, and whom she felt inspired to copy or parody; and how in turn the real Potter has inspired the recent spate of false 'Potters'. In the last twenty years there has been a proliferation of exhibitions, and new facilities for display: showcases, special rooms, and even whole buildings. In Cumbria the Heelis Gallery, Hawkshead, was inaugurated by the National Trust in July 1988, and in August 1997 the Armitt Trust in Ambleside moved to its first proper home. At the end of 1989 the Linder Collection joined the Victoria and Albert Museum's other Potter collections at Blythe House, Olympia, London. A special Beatrix Potter Study Room, with an inner room for displays, opened at the Book Trust, Wandsworth, South London, in October 1997. Catalogues and lists, articles and books have all benefited since 1987 from a greatly improved quality of reproduction, thanks to Potter's publisher, Frederick Warne.

In 1984 I wrote: 'It is likely . . . that more privately-owned hoards will come to light as the [interest in Potter] gains momentum. . . . The existence of an important collection seems to act as a magnet, attracting other benefactors and encouraging them to give treasures to what they assume must be a good home'. Increased publicity, especially the publicity which accompanies high-profile exhibitions, brings forth yet more of Beatrix Potter's work. The fact that so much of her *œuvre*, in contrast to that of Arthur Rackham for instance, is concentrated in public or quasi-public collections does encourage some private individuals to give or bequeath their treasures to the nation. In so doing they reap a considerable tax advantage, but owners are naturally tempted by today's much inflated values to sell instead. We may deplore rising prices, but at least they have induced more owners to offer on the open market drawings which may eventually enter the public domain: the fine collection of Lloyd Cotsen, for example, is destined for Princeton. Curators and collectors alike must be vigilant, scanning sale catalogues, listening to trade gossip, and maintaining a private information network.

The V&A's collections have been enriched partly by gift or bequest, and partly by loan. In 1983 Joan Duke presented a group of Rupert Potter's photographs. The Linder Collection, property of the Linder Trust, came to the V&A on long loan at the end of 1989, and the 'Peter Rabbit Picture Letter', property of Pearson plc, in 1991. In 1996 Lucie Carr (the Lucie of *The Tale of Mrs. Tiggy-Winkle*) gave the Museum her collection of miniature letters, a rare coloured picture-letter, and some first editions. Sadly, her inscribed dedication copy of *The Tale of Mrs. Tiggy-Winkle* had been stolen not long before. In 1997 the Museum acquired the collection of Beatrix Potter's niece, Nancy Nicholson (Mrs Hudson); this included the manuscript of an unpublished tale, 'The Oakmen', illustrated in colour, and a previously unknown picture-letter.

The Beatrix Potter Showcase at the V&A celebrated in its April-August 2000 display 'The Beatrix Potter Society, 1980-2000', bringing together several of the Society's acquisitions now on loan to the V&A, including the 1905 *Holiday Diary* and the recently purchased sepia drawing of 'Duchess in Sawrey'. Another of the Society's treasures, the Hildesheimer & Faulkner Greetings Card bought at Sotheby's on 19 May 1994, was included in the first display of the new V&A showcase.

From my privileged position as Curator of the V&A's Potter collections, I am sometimes able to alert relevant institutions to items as they appear in catalogues, or even before. In this way, the Armitt managed in 1991 to secure from Sotheby's 'Long-eared bats disputing with a common bat for possession of the roosting place, drawn from tame animals'. I next contrived to put in their way some important microscopic drawings, dated from 1896 to 1898, from a mixed lot at Christie's South Kensington in January 1994. That lot also included an interesting group of letters to Edmund Potter from the great Radical politician Richard Cobden. Also in 1994, with help from the National Art Collections Fund, the Armitt acquired a fine study of newts. Prices for natural history subjects tend to be surprisingly reasonable compared with those for fantasy rabbits! All the collections have benefited from recent advances in Potter studies, and all have embarked on conservation projects: the Armitt, the Frederick Warne Archive, the National Trust, the V&A, and, in America, the Free Library of Philadelphia. Increased knowledge inevitably brings with it a greater concern about the vulnerability of drawings, and hence more restrictions on their display. Acid-free materials are always used now, from solander boxes to tissue guards; unmounted drawings are encased in special polyester sleeves (melinex or secol). Metal storage cabinets are now favoured. Levels of humidity, temperature and ultra-violet radiation are regularly monitored. Light levels for display have to be restricted, since exposure to light causes immediate deterioration and the V&A has now introduced a light policy for works of art on paper, prompted in particular by the repeated demand for certain key objects. For the V&A, any external exhibition venue has to be vetted by the Government Security Adviser for all aspects of security.

The Beatrix Potter Society has been especially generous in funding various conservation projects, at the V&A and elsewhere. Picture-letters and miniature letters from the Linder Bequest have been rehoused using the 'Lilliput' system, and a fragile fungus painting has now been restored. Thanks to a recent grant, work can begin on new storage and conservation for the collection of Potter photographs.

Beatrix Potter's publishers, Frederick Warne, have made a considerable contribution to the care of original materials, not least in sponsoring, since February 1990, a full-time Frederick Warne Curatorship, and in supporting their own Archive. By photographing every available image, they have created a comprehensive Visual Archive, invaluable not just as a commercial tool, but as a source for their innovative exhibition programme, which recognises the problems in displaying any work on paper. As owners of the twenty-six paintings from *The Tale of Peter Rabbit*, which everyone wants to borrow, they are particularly conscious of these limitations. High-quality reproductions now make it possible, however, to take displays to many more venues, and more often. Controversial, by contrast, are Warne's 'collected' editions, the animated films, and the resulting books which use the artwork from these animations, purporting to be 'Beatrix Potter'. One may argue that the animations, in particular, actually divert new generations away from the delights of Potter's original pictures and format.

The Enid Linder Foundation has supported Potter studies in many ways. The Foundation's generosity to the Beatrix Potter Society is well known; it has also provided a new display case for the Book Trust, and has funded the Beatrix

Potter Showcase at the V&A, so making possible changing exhibitions in the Museum. The Enid Linder Foundation has also contributed to the production costs of the new Linder Collection Catalogue and has contribued more than half towards the cost of conserving and mounting all the drawings in that Collection.

All recent work has relied on the firm foundations of Leslie Linder's pioneering researches and meticulous records, and on the results of his detective work in tracking down Potter originals. I was very glad to have had the opportunity in 1999 to honour 'Beatrix Potter and Leslie Linder' in an exhibition at the V&A. Though a highly cultured man, Linder was not a specialist in the field of children's literature or book illustration. Most major displays of Potter's work up to 1972 were drawn from Linder's collections or arranged by him. The V&A exhibition of 1972-73, organised by Irene Whalley and Celia O'Malley, was the first to set Beatrix Potter in context. Since then, even when concentrating on *The Tale of Peter Rabbit*, exhibitors have felt obliged to adopt this broader approach.

Over the last twenty-five years the emphasis has altered in other ways too. Most important is a new appreciation of Potter as a scientific illustrator of insects, fungi and fossils, as well as of archaeological artefacts. Experts from the Natural History Museum, London, from Edinburgh and from Kew, on first seeing her microscopic drawings, have all been amazed by their beauty and accuracy, for instance, the 1886 study of Zooids (marine animals) on seaweed.

It is common knowledge today that Beatrix Potter often used to re-draw her designs, and many more of these variants have now come to light. The 'knitting mouse' motif, for instance, exists in several versions, one in *Appley Dapply's Nursery Rhymes*, and another, in an unusually bright pink palette, as a home-made Greetings Card for Christmas 1900 (see Chris Beetles, *The Illustrators*, 1991, inside front cover). Her 'Garden at Tenby', in the Linder Bequest (LB 467), a background for *The Tale of Peter Rabbit*, has only recently been linked with another

A variant of the Mouse Knitting, used as a home-made Greetings Card for Christmas 1900

One of several versions of 'Cinderella's Carriage', this one is in the Linder Bequest

version hanging at Hill Top, but described only as 'Spring' in the National Trust listing. Version 1 of 'Cinderella's Carriage' is in the Linder Bequest; version 2 was sold at Sotheby's on 19 May 1994, and version 3, dated 1899 (Sotheby's, 30 November 1994), is inscribed 'for Mr. Warne with kind regards July 25th 05' (the day of Beatrix and Norman's engagement). The latter is the only variant to include stag beetles, and appears to be the most finished of the three.

Variant book pictures exist also, often apparently because the publisher asked for new compositions in which the animal figures were more prominent. Working on the Tate Gallery and Pierpont Morgan Library exhibitions in 1987, we became aware of many unused 'alternatives'. Some are in the National Trust collection, such as a variant from *The Tale of Pigling Bland*, in which much more of Beatrix Potter herself appears. Sometimes, but not always, the new composition is an improvement. Early editions of *The Tale of Benjamin Bunny* reveal two variants of one design (for the second version, see 1987 edition, p.11). In the first version Benjamin is less prominent, blending into the woodland background as part of an altogether more pleasing whole.

A sketch for the 'Rabbit Postman', from the Linder Bequest

Beatrix Potter also often recycled her images, but not every lineage has been traced. One new discovery, sold to a private collector at Christie's South Kensington in 1995, is the rabbit brandishing a letter and a tricorne hat. This finished

32

watercolour, linked with a related sketch from the Linder Bequest (LB 1766), was included in the inaugural display of the V&A Showcase. A rather similar rabbit postman features in Greetings Cards, both early and late, one with Gwaynynog as backdrop. The July picture in *Peter Rabbit's Almanac for 1929* revives the 'rabbit as piper' scene of 'The Rabbits' Christmas Party'. Two variants are known of the grey-toned rabbit with trug and fork, an image which reappears in colour as the *Almanac's* frontispiece: one is in the Linder Bequest (LB 1011), and another came to light at Sotheby's in November 1995. Three variants have been discovered so far of 'The Rabbit's Dream': one in the Linder Bequest, one in the Linder

A variant of the 'Rabbit with trug and fork', sold at Sotheby's, 2 November 1995

Collection, and one privately owned. The anti-hero of a pictorial sequence about the guinea pig with toothache (scene 1) is reborn as Tuppenny in *The Fairy Caravan*.

A pencil sketch from the Linder Bequest, showing Old Mr Bunny smoking against a kitchen background

Backgrounds too are adapted to suit the subject. We all know the 'Gentlemen Rabbits', comfortably smoking and drinking on a settle by the hearth. In the Linder Bequest is a pencil sketch of Old Mr. Bunny in the same kitchen, complete with rabbit tiles (LB 821); and in the National Trust collection there is a watercolour version, signed 'HBP'. Sketching the main staircase at Bedwell Lodge in 1891, Beatrix altered its dimensions slightly to improve the composition. So, too, the back passage at Bedwell Lodge is more cramped in reality. Re-using this background for 'The Mice in their Store-room', Beatrix altered it even more. Similar panelling confirms the date of the 'Appley Dapply' rhyme sequence as 1891.

Beatrix Potter's versatility never fails to surprise us and she tried out a variety of techniques. Her 'brief flirtation with oils' is well documented. The mysterious 'Mrs. A.' who taught her is still not identified, but she may have been Mrs. Sophie Anderson. A hitherto unknown group of drawings in fine pen-and-ink came to light at a recent sale at Christie's South Kensington (12 January 1994, lots 144-145); but probably more are by Bertram than by Beatrix. A few years ago one could buy a replica of 'Kep', the original of which she had exquisitely modelled in clay in 1907. Apart from schoolroom work, no other clay modellings by Beatrix are known.

Only a little more information is now available about the materials that Potter used. A paintbox which she had owned at the age of fourteen, now on long loan to the V&A, once contained in its drawer her student notes on colours used in flower drawing. Later in life, she rarely mentions such *minutiæ*. It has been suggested that the velvety effect achieved in 'Three Little Mice Sat Down to Spin', for example, is due to dense pencil lines beneath the colour. Examination under the microscope however reveals only a characteristic light underdrawing. The texture comes entirely from a fine-pointed brush used with very dry pigment.

Looking closely at the incomplete sketches, often on the versos of other drawings, we learn yet more about Potter's working methods. Relatively few of the fungus drawings, for instance, survive in an unfinished state. These reveal that, as in her book pictures, the background is drawn first, and the main figure – fungus or face – is put in last. How fast did Beatrix Potter work? Probably quite fast, as in the case of landscape sketches such as some surprisingly avant-garde examples of around 1910, now in the Free Library of Philadelphia. The Free Library also owns a timed drawing of a rabbit, inscribed '20 minutes', but this sort of information is the exception, not the rule.

Just as in Beatrix Potter's *Journal* and in her books we hear borrowed voices, so too we see borrowings in her art. The picture shows a German Jemima in poke bonnet and shawl, from *Hanne Nüte un de lütte Pudel*, a folktale illustrated after Otto Speckter in 1865. Also by Speckter is *Der gestiefelte Kater*, which must have influenced Potter's 'Puss-in-Boots'. Fairy tale

A wood-engraving after Otto Speckter, from Fritz Reuter, *Hanne Nüte un de lütte Pudel*, 1865

34

Beatrix Potter's version of a boy on the back of a mouse, and the original picture in Charlotte Yonge's *The History of Sir Thomas Thumb*, 1855

designs by Otto Speckter and Ludwig Richter also served her as models for practice in architectural and figure drawing; one study is inscribed 'Copy from a woodcut by Ludwig Richter', though the floral border is her own. It has become more evident that much of Potter's juvenile work was actually copied, and not just the schoolroom exercises. Some of those were taken from outline drawings in Vere Foster's series of drawing manuals: buildings, trees and flowers; baskets and a waterbutt; mammals and birds. Vere Foster is the main source for her transfer prints (LB 104-107), and for the designs painted by Rupert Potter on plates for the nursery at Bolton Gardens, which are now at Hill Top.

The young Beatrix copied several plates from the bird books of Jemima Blackburn, a distinguished Scottish artist whom she much admired. I have discovered that a page design in her 1876 drawing book (LB 1093) is taken from *The Pipits* (1872), one of Blackburn's humorous books for children. Last year I traced another source. A rather undistinguished drawing of a boy on mouse-back, dated 1896 (LC 21/A/4; cat.5.8), is inspired by a picture in Charlotte Yonge's *The History of Sir Thomas Thumb* (1855); the same boy and mouse appear in a picture-letter sent to Noel Moore on 6 April 1896. Again the illustrator is Jemima Blackburn. No doubt other Blackburn-Potter links are still to be found.

Conscious verbal parody is a common phenomenon in Beatrix Potter's *Journal*. Visual parody, too, occurs more commonly in Potter's art than has previously been realised. Leslie Linder already knew of 'Cupboard Love' by Briton Rivière, a depiction of Beatrix's cousin Kate with a dog, as the model for Duchess in *The Tale of the Pie and the Patty-Pan*. Rivière's painting was last heard of when it was acquired by a J. or I. Dole, for one thousand and fifty guineas, at the sale of Edmund Crompton Potter's collection (Christie, Manson and Wood, 22 March 1884); it has not been seen since. Conflicting suggestions, both plausible, have been put forward for the image which inspired 'Peter began to cry'. More recently, Selwyn Goodacre remarked on the familiar look of some playing kittens in Henry Holiday's illustration for 'Fit the Fifth' of Lewis Carroll's *Hunting of the Snark* (1876).

Immediately popular, the pictures for the little books have always been imitated or copied, whether for pleasure or for profit. Inflated prices and publicity make faking increasingly worthwhile, and so it becomes increasingly important to identify the real thing. An immediate instinctive reaction tends to be quite reliable, so long as it is informed by experience. Experience in turn helps to develop 'eye': the more genuine works one can see, the better. Objective analysis is also essential, however. The component features of a drawing must be identified: motifs and details; how particular features have been treated (eyes and ears especially, in the case of Potter); the type of background; a feeling of movement, or its absence; likewise, medium and technique; the use of colour; how any corrections have been made. Comparison with authentic works can be instructive. Monograms or signatures, lettering plain or decorative, all must be carefully scrutinised. Some of the cleverest copies in colour are let down by the quality of the draughtsmanship. Potter is remarkable above all for the anatomical accuracy and solidity of her figures: in her own words, they 'stand on their legs . . . well'. Finally, provenance has to be checked carefully: even if superficially convincing, it can prove a trap for the unwary.

Many copies are obvious. Some are competently executed but are clearly not by Beatrix Potter. Some are more problematical, like the Greetings Card design illustrated on the back cover of a Bonhams catalogue (16 December 1997). Motif and composition are completely convincing, but the technique, though quite accomplished, is rather less so. The picture compares unfavourably with 'November' in *Peter Rabbit's Almanac for 1929* and with a related pair of Christmas Card designs in the National Trust collection. A safe identification can be particularly difficult in the case of the printed silk doylies which have lately flooded the market.

36

Even now, some private owners of works by Potter do not fully realise the importance of the material, or else have simply forgotten that they have it. Even institutions can be similarly unaware. Many years ago, Elizabeth Battrick had to remind the National Trust that they held the original pen-and-ink drawings for the privately printed *The Tale of Peter Rabbit*. In 1970 Enid Linder remarked of a fine toy picture that it 'did not sell'; another toy picture ('Mrs Rabbit and Son/Rabbit Greengrocer') surfaced at Sotheby's in June 1985, selling for only £8,800. Since 1991 however, toy pictures have been valued at anything between £15,000 and £30,000, depending on their quality. The 'Peter Rabbit Picture-Letter', kept in a bank vault since it was sold at Sotheby's by Margaret Lane in 1947, came to light after forty years as a result of a major exhibition at the Tate Gallery. Seven years later a group of twenty-five long-lost picture-letters from that same 1947 sale were found in an attic and were auctioned by Woolley and Wallis on 28 June 1994. Rediscovered in Lucie Carr's collection was a rare coloured picture-letter, dated 24 August 1904.

The most exciting reappearance for me was the discovery, at the house of family friends, of 'A Dream of Toasted Cheese', drawn in 1899 for Sir Henry Roscoe. It was reproduced as a plate both in Roscoe's *Memoirs* (1906) and in early editions of Margaret Lane's *The Tale of Beatrix Potter*. My most exciting <u>new</u> discovery was the missing design for verse 2 of 'Appley Dapply'. It was brought in to the V&A, again as a direct result of publicity for the Tate exhibition, by a lady who had been given it as a child in the 1930s. When Beatrix Potter had to provide illustrations for a rhyme book in 1917, in a hurry, she must have temporarily mislaid this design. Instead, she produced a substitute which, being in her contemporary style, was quite different. The rediscovered original version was sold at Sotheby's in 1996 to Thomas Schuster. Few people know that the large Renier Collection of Children's Books, which moved back to South Kensington in November 2000 from the Bethnal Green Museum of Childhood, includes two Potter drawings: a study of ducks in chalk, and a watercolour of 'Newlands from Swinside'. Sotheby's sale of 18 November 1999 featured the only known complete set of 'This little pig went to market', done for Stephanie Hyde Parker and dated 18 November 1899.

'Discovery' can also simply mean looking at the artwork with new eyes and making new connections. More images are now available to us to help with identification. This is especially true of the scientific illustrations, but applies also to lesser mysteries such as 'Who stole the tarts?': four tarts and a cake on blue-rimmed plates, and a green bottle with two glasses (LB 1775). It was intended for a Greetings Card, and now appears to be related to the 'Appley Dapply' designs.

'*Who stole the tarts?*' a design from the Linder Bequest

Now that we are more aware of Potter's fungus subjects, we notice more examples of fungi in her fantasy drawings. Intriguingly, a different species of fungus is depicted in a preliminary sketch for 'The Toads' Tea Party' from that in the finished watercolour. An unpublished rhyme, 'Nid nid noddy, we stand in a ring', recalls a lyrical passage in the *Journal*, describing a host of mushrooms (17 November 1896). Its accompanying illustration has more resonance for us now.

Camouflaged among the shells in an unusual still life given to Nellie Warne (LC 16/A/5; cat.3.73) are two Japanese *netsuke* of masks, comic and tragic. Oriental scholars have identified them as representations of the Shinto goddess Okame, or of a female character portrayed in the *No* drama. While Beatrix Potter rarely drew figures or faces, the Linder Bequest includes a surprisingly good caricature (LB 691), which new photographic evidence encourages us to believe was of her mother.

In the Linder Archive I found a note in Leslie Linder's hand referring to 'Parton's boy', whom Beatrix Potter used as model for the seated Tailor in *The Tailor of Gloucester*. It seems that she photographed Parton's daughter in the Nuttery at Harescombe Grange, Gloucestershire, dressed as Red Riding Hood. By analogy it is clear that a photograph in the Cotsen Collection served as exemplar for two pictures of Red Riding Hood in a ruched bonnet (now in the Free Library of Philadelphia), since they date from August 1894, when the

Potters were staying in the Scottish Borders. Places and people are being identified for the first time, such as Harescombe Grange; Melford Hall; Bedwell Lodge; Derwent Cottage, Winchelsea. 'The China Shepherdess' from Philadelphia, a design for a Hans Andersen fairy tale, includes the figure of a china chimney-sweep. Comparison with sketches in the Linder Collection identifies the setting as Derwent Cottage: the same pair of bellows appears, and the same china figures.

Curators and collectors do sometimes make mistakes. Linder described one particularly fine pen drawing as 'Study of a horse's (?) skull' (LB 702). When my mother saw it and remarked: 'I shouldn't care to bridle that horse', I looked again more carefully. It is the skull of a wolf! The 'Tarantula', as it was formerly described, again from the Philadelphia collection, is actually a much magnified 'Jumping spider'. We need to enlist experts to identify fauna, flora, fungi, fossils, archaeological artefacts or Japanese *netsuke*.

Plenty of mysteries remain, not least the current whereabouts of known drawings. Furthermore, several 'new' items have been found, but information about them often has to remain strictly confidential. By 'known' I mean artworks that have reappeared only to vanish again. Rupert Potter's London

Beatrix Potter as caricaturist: possibly a sketch
of Mrs Potter

39

photographs, deposited at the Civic Trust, were seen there and then promptly lost. Even more important from the art-historical standpoint are Rupert Potter's photographs of portraits by Millais, some taken at several different stages of their creation. Prints of these photographs used to hang on the walls of the Linder drawing room at Buckhurst Hill, where they were seen by Michael Harvey in the course of his research into the Potter-Millais connection. They have not been seen since. Leslie Linder's *The Art of Beatrix Potter*, p. 110, reproduces a handsome study of furze (*Ulex*), inscribed 'Sidmouth 1902'. This painting formerly belonged to the Hunt Institute, but was sold on 21 November 1986 at Christie's New York, together with the Hunt's entire collection of eighteen watercolours, mainly botanical subjects. I have been able to trace only a few items from that sale; others were immediately sold on or given away. Also in Linder's *Art* is a painting done in Long Melford, entitled 'On the road to Bury St Edmunds'. It is one of two drawings apparently lost or stolen while on loan to the Grey Art Gallery, New York, in Spring 1977.

The famous 'fishing frog' picture, intended for the 1905 'Book of Rhymes' is stylistically very close to 'A Snail and its young', dated June 26 – July 28, 1898 (Sotheby, 7-8 July 1990; see also Chris Beetles, *The Illustrators*, 1991, p.31), in which the Snail peers at its egg through a magnifying glass. The Snail, like Version 3 of 'Cinderella', may now be in some private collection, unless it is lying unsold in a dealer's vaults. A twin to this design, also dated July 1898 and with a very similar composition, is entitled 'Whimsical snail burying eggs and cow bugs'. It was included in the 1966 Philadelphia exhibition, but does not belong to the Free Library collection. An obvious connection can be made with the snail's nest in a picture-letter sent to Freda Moore on 30 July 1898. Surely this is the snail in one of Potter's unpublished rhymes:

There was an old snail with a nest –
Who very great terror expressed,
Lest the wood-lice all round
In the cracks under-ground
Should eat up her eggs in that nest!

Besides these 'unknown' drawings, only recently discovered, there are drawings known only by repute. The recipient of the missing 'Appley Dapply' picture had also been given some alphabet designs and an unusually large and elaborate card in celebration of her wedding. All except 'Appley Dapply' were wrecked by water damage in World War II. Even now one hears of material which has been thrown away; and much more must have been lost or destroyed. I am sorry to say that a former owner of some important microscopic studies of spore development, conveniently done on card, cut them up for markers. Leslie Linder re-attached the fragments by backing them with another sheet, but some pieces have been lost.

Several pictures for *The Tailor of Gloucester* were lost during Beatrix Potter's lifetime. Another book picture which has disappeared more recently is the pen-and-ink study of a handsome Herdwick ram at the head of Troutbeck, one of the *Fairy Caravan* series in the Frederick Warne Archive. Many more drawings are doubtless waiting to be found again.

There is still work in progress, and much unfinished business. The catalogue of the Linder Bequest had to be published before inaccuracies could be eliminated and before much new information could be incorporated. It urgently

A snail peers at its egg through a magnifying glass

41

needs to be corrected, revised and expanded, to the standard of the new Linder Collection Catalogue. The Linder Archive has never been catalogued in detail. A fuller scrutiny of Leslie Linder's notebooks and letters is likely to throw light on the provenance of drawings in his collections.

The outstanding thesis by Janie Coitit-Godfrey ('Le Monde de Beatrix Potter', University of Bordeaux, 1988) should be seen as a standard work on Potter, and therefore needs to be translated into English. The author discusses text, image, and their synthesis in 'L'imaginaire de Beatrix Potter', with many thought-provoking insights, and a characteristically French combination of theory and lucidity. Charts and diagrams clarify the argument; one, for instance, analyses the 'Interrelation of the *Tales*', and another demonstrates the 'Narrative dynamic of the illustrations in *Peter Rabbit*'.

A new edition of Judy Taylor's *That Naughty Rabbit* is scheduled for 2002. Perhaps it is time to plan a set of short monographs dealing with the genesis of each *Tale*, bringing together all the available artwork, from early sketches to finished watercolours, unpublished variants included. A start has been made on the systematic analysis of all the rhyme illustrations.

Researchers and students, in or out of schools and colleges, are now addressing a much greater variety of projects, as for example the relationship between Dürer's hare and Potter's rabbits; her portrayal of spinning wheels and of pigs; and, most popular of all, her recycling of images. Some commentators place on these pictures a greater burden than they can possibly bear, yet fail to notice the parody on which they are frequently based. Pioneering work in all these fields was done before 1980, but several special areas have not yet been fully investigated, such as the scientific illustrations, or techniques and materials. Inaccuracies must be corrected and loose ends tied up. There is still detective work to be done.

Over these last twenty years, collections have been consolidated. They are better cared for, have become more accessible and their contents are displayed in catalogues. Selections of their contents are aired in frequent exhibitions and displays. Monographs and articles have proliferated, especially thanks to the Beatrix Potter Society. But the ever-increasing interest in Potter's work has led to greater acquisitiveness and higher prices. We have become more conscious of Beatrix Potter's productivity, her versatility and her perfectionism. Above all, we now realise her greatness as an artist of natural history.

REFERENCES

In order to assist the smooth reading of this article, most of the references supplied in the text have been removed. All the important ones will be found in the bibliography below. Should the reader require more specific details, these can be supplied by the author, Anne Stevenson Hobbs (c/o Museum Archives (The National Art Library), Blythe House, 23 Blythe Road, Olympia, London W14 0QF).

Hobbs, A.S. and J.I. Whalley, *Beatrix Potter: The V & A Collection*, Victoria and Albert Museum & F. Warne, 1985

Hobbs, A.S., *Beatrix Potter's Art*, F. Warne, 1989

Jay, E., M. Noble and A.S. Hobbs, *A Victorian Naturalist: Beatrix Potter's Drawings from the Armitt Collection*, F. Warne, 1992

Lane, M., *The Magic Years of Beatrix Potter*, F. Warne, 1978

Linder, L., *A History of the Writings of Beatrix Potter*, F. Warne, 1971

Moore, A.C., *The Art of Beatrix Potter*, with an appreciation by A.C.M., and notes to each section by E. and L. Linder, revised edition, F. Warne, 1972

Taylor, J., *Beatrix Potter, Artist, Storyteller and Countrywoman*, F. Warne, 1986

Beatrix Potter and Hill Top (an illustrated souvenir), The National Trust, 1989

Letters to Children from Beatrix Potter, collected and introduced by J.T., F. Warne, 1992

Taylor, J., J.I. Whalley, A.S. Hobbs and E.M. Battrick, *Beatrix Potter, 1866 - 1943: The Artist and her World*, F. Warne & The National Trust, 1987

Abbreviations: LB Linder Bequest; LC Linder Collection. Both of these are now housed in the Victoria and Albert Museum.

A number of works discussed in this article have also been dealt with in various issues of the Beatrix Potter Society's *Newsletter*, to which indexes are available.

Pieces of the Jigsaw – Beatrix Potter's Art in the United States: Exhibitions, Collections and Popular Media

BETSY BRAY

WHILE CHILDREN may have been the initial audience for Beatrix Potter's work, interest in her now extends far beyond those origins. Since her death in 1943, Beatrix Potter's work has become celebrated and transformed in ways that the author herself could never have imagined when she privately published *The Tale of Peter Rabbit* in 1901. The artistry of Beatrix Potter has traveled during the past century from the bedside story of children into American museums, the popular media and all the way to the Internet. There have been interactive exhibits, new formats for her stories, and special editions of her original line-block drawings. Peter Rabbit himself has transcended his literary origins to become an icon of popular culture to stand alongside Mickey Mouse and Pokemon.

Beatrix Potter could not possibly have expected her audience to become as vast and diverse as the population of the United States. And just as the United States is a mosaic of many cultures, so we can see that the many ways in which her artistic genius has been exhibited in America is something like a jigsaw puzzle – a puzzle with various pieces that speak to the interests of many different Americans. A very important piece of the jigsaw is the exhibition. While a reader can only experience Beatrix Potter through her art and words within the context of a tale, an exhibition can bring together numerous pieces of her life and so share the extent of her work's creativity and precision with the public. The exhibit has also provided museum curators and Beatrix Potter enthusiasts with the challenge of packaging Potter for a media-savvy generation. One of the most ambitious Beatrix Potter exhibitions in the United States is the touring interactive exhibit designed by Philadelphia's Academy of Natural Sciences. In

44

'The World of Peter Rabbit – the Art and Science of Beatrix Potter', Americans can experience the natural world which she celebrated in her art. The show includes Potter's original renderings of fungi, insects, mammals and birds. But that is not all. There are also readings of her stories, live animals, a re-creation of Mr. McGregor's garden complete with giant vegetables, a computer game where users can try to decipher the secret code in Beatrix Potter's *Journal*, and even Victorian clothes for dress-up games.

The exhibit is structured so that the very act of walking through the gallery becomes a story itself. The excitement begins at the entrance, where visitors step through an English garden gate and enter the world according to Peter Rabbit. Along the wall, colorful reproductions of Beatrix Potter's drawings tell the story, while a bird's chirping is heard in the distance. A six-foot-tall watering-can beckons the visitor to enter and explore. Luckily, this one is dry and comfortable inside. The huge tree – home to Peter, his mother and three sisters – is also complete with teapot and a fireplace. Just as the large replicas let visitors share Peter Rabbit's world, activities help showcase Beatrix Potter's extraordinary work as a naturalist and artist in the Victorian Gallery. Would-be artists can even try their own hands at scientific illustration.

Since it opened in 1992, 'The World of Peter Rabbit' has been so successful that it continues to travel to cities around the country. Dallas, Pittsburgh and St. Paul have all played host to the exhibition, and smaller cities have also been included in its itinerary. The success of the exhibition has also inspired increased academic activity around Beatrix Potter. When the exhibition was shown in the Santa Barbara Museum of Natural History in August 1994, Jeanne Quick of San Diego, California, organized a wonderful Beatrix Potter Conference in conjunction with it. Over one hundred people attended that Conference entitled 'The Nature of Peter Rabbit'.

In order to keep the eight-year-old exhibit fresh, programs have been continually updated and added even as it travels around the United States. Sometimes it is the venue itself which adapts the exhibition. In 1993, the Director of the Seattle Science Center saw the exhibition of natural history drawings as a special opportunity to get younger visitors interested in science. The great accuracy of Potter's scientific illustrations has earned them the respect of naturalists and botanists. They also provide a marvelous link between Potter's delightful fiction and the natural world from which she drew her inspiration.

In South Carolina, the artwork of Beatrix Potter became the jumping-off point for activities that ranged from a documentary on the life of Potter to musings on English gardening in Potter's time. In this manner, the exhibit became less about the literary properties that brought her fame, than about her remarkable life.

Even if you were more interested in carrot cultivation than Potter's characters, there was still something in the exhibit to enjoy and learn from.

Special one-time exhibitions have also brought Beatrix Potter's work to a wider public. In New York City, the Pierpont Morgan Library held the exhibition entitled 'Beatrix Potter: Artist and Storyteller' in 1988. A highlight of this exhibition was the display of 300 watercolors and other memorabilia. Attendees were also able to view the original drawings for *The Tale of Peter Rabbit* and *The Tailor of Gloucester*. Speakers such as Judy Taylor discussed Potter as a young artist and the early influences on her art.

Because the Free Library of Philadelphia owns the largest public collection of Beatrix Potter's work outside Great Britain, it is only fitting that Philadelphia has often been the venue for events celebrating her art. In 1999, the Free Library's Rare Book Department was the site of 'Beatrix Potter's Animal Friends', an exhibition of original sketches and watercolors. Included were the original illustrations for *The Tailor of Gloucester* and *The Tale of Little Pig Robinson*. A symposium entitled: 'Beatrix Potter Perspectives From Here And Abroad' was held in conjunction with the exhibition, attended by sixty people, and sponsored by the Free Library of Philadelphia's Rare Book Department and the Beatrix Potter Society. In November 1992, the Free Library's Elkins Room also played host to the first Beatrix Potter Conference in the United States and a symposium was held with the Academy of Natural Sciences, which showcased the exhibition 'Peter Rabbit, and Friends'. The joint exhibition from the Free Library and the Academy was called 'Peter Rabbit on the Parkway'. One hundred participants heard Potter scholars Jane Morse, Karen Lightner and Judy Taylor speak. As part of the exhibition, a book, *Beatrix Potter: A Guide to the Collection of the Rare Book Department, Free Library of Philadelphia* was produced.

Just as you might find Peter Rabbit nibbling on a vegetable in

The Longwood Gardens in Pennsylvania displayed two figures from *The Tale of Pigling Bland* as part of their 1998 chrysanthemum festival

the shady corner of a garden, Beatrix Potter herself was a fixture at local agricultural fairs. More than a few gardeners have paid tribute to this gentlewoman farmer in a fitting manner. In 1998, the Longwood Gardens in Kennett Square, Pennsylvania, were the setting for a chrysanthemum festival with the theme 'Peter Rabbit and Friends in the Garden'. Gardeners created more than two dozen imaginative topiaries based on the characters from Potter's books; the characters were then placed throughout twenty different indoor gardens that had been fashioned to depict favorite scenes from the classic Potter stories. Karen Lightner, Beatrix Potter Curator from the Free Library of Philadelphia, and I, both had the opportunity to give presentations about Beatrix Potter there as part of the show. Also on display at Longwood Gardens were reproductions of Potter's landscapes, botanical drawings and animal studies, as well as Royal Doulton figurines of characters from the stories.

Flower shows have also displayed Potter's art in a sympathetic setting. In Minneapolis in 1998, the Dayton-Bachman flower show was titled 'Beatrix Potter's A Storybook Spring' and provided an even more ambitious tribute to Potter. This show not only brought together characters from her stories, but a reproduction of the landscape near her Hill Top home. According to the event's production manager, the show was designed to achieve a Lake District look, 'less formal, kind of overgrown, mossy and kind of lush'. That rustic aim did not rule out the use of technology since it included as sets Mr McGregor's garden gate, and a vegetable garden raided by an animated Peter Rabbit.

As many enthusiastic collectors of Potter-abilia are only too aware, the little books have inspired all kinds of merchandise associated with the stories and characters. Other exhibitions have been dedicated solely towards displaying specific products that have evolved from Potter's art. In 1993 in Saint Louis, Wedgwood china decorated with the characters from *The Tale of Peter Rabbit* was included with the Masterpiece Collection display, a special traveling exhibit of ornate Wedgwood china.

But the newest exhibition space for Potter's work is not a museum, but in cyberspace. In 1999 a virtual exhibition by *The Horn Book* became available to the public through the Internet. With a click of a mouse, you can see Potter letters, as well as a copy of her verse and illustrations. These items can be viewed at *The Horn Book* web site (www.hbook.com). It is interesting to note that *The Horn Book*, a children's literature magazine, was once edited by Beatrix Potter's good friend, Bertha Mahony. In addition, the Ohio University Telecommunications Center in Athens, Ohio, has also included some of Potter's illustrated stories on its web site (www.tcom.ohiou.edu). This site allows you to read *The Tale of Peter Rabbit* and look at each illustration on a computer screen, while the story is read to you through the speakers hooked up to your computer. The irony that Potter's art, depicting so much of the natural world, is now available in cyberspace does not detract from the importance of these events. In fact, it is exciting to know that the pictures and words of Beatrix Potter can now be appreciated by anyone with a personal computer and access to the World Wide Web.

After exhibitions, the other most significant piece of the American jigsaw of appreciation is through the private collection. However, the nature of private collections being what it is, opportunities to see the art of Beatrix Potter in this context are usually very limited. We have been fortunate that during the past few years, partly through auctions, several significant collections in the United States have become available for viewing.

On 16 April 1997, Christie's East in New York auctioned off a Beatrix Potter collection owned by Doris Frohnsdorff. This impressive collection, amassed over thirty years, included drawings, rare publications like *Our Dear Relations*, first editions in their original dust jackets, letters, photographs, figurines, and toys. Many of the books available for bidding had been signed or inscribed by Potter or by Noel Moore, the boy for whom *The Tale of Peter Rabbit* was originally written. While some Beatrix Potter fans only got the chance to see these lots in the showroom, they were very popular with buyers. In all, 311 items were auctioned in a period of four hours. There were several pieces of art auctioned off such as 'The Three Witches of Birnam Wood' (sold for $11,500), 'Camfield Beauty' ($3,680) and 'Berries Study' ($3,450). During this auction, the Beatrix Potter Society purchased for $12,000 'Duchess in Sawrey', a fine original pen-and-wash drawing that was intended for *The Tale of the Pie and the Patty-Pan*. While the identity of the other buyers is confidential, we can probably assume that the collection was sold to many private collectors, librarians and curators of other collections, among them the well-known collector Lloyd E. Cotsen, founder and former Chief Operating Officer of the Neutrogena Corporation of Los Angeles. He has built up an impressive collection of Beatrix Potter art, letters, signed first editions and photographs.

Ivy Trent, Librarian of the Cotsen Library in Los Angeles, explains: 'The goal of the collection is to provide a resource for scholars of childhood and childhood education, to serve as a point of contact between the world of scholarship and the world of childhood, and to foster literacy, creativity and joy in learning'. A portion of Cotsen's Children's Collection – which includes 50,000 items ranging over the last 400 years – was given to Princeton University with the Cotsen Children's Library opening there in 1998. One of the Potter items of particular interest is the 'Peter Rabbit mechanical in watercolor' (a moveable toy), containing one of the earliest pictures of Peter Rabbit in color. There are drawings of Peter Rabbit on two sides of the toy: in one, Peter is giving flowers to a rabbit through the window of a house; on the other, he is taking carrots to the Flopsy Bunnies. Also included in Cotsen's collection are the illustrations for *The Tale of the Pie and the Patty-Pan*.

New Potter discoveries are being made all the time as more private collections are being put on display. In the spring of 1999, visitors to the Perrot Memorial Library in Old Greenwich, Connecticut, saw original Potter art that was part of a never-before-shown private collection. The exhibition, entitled 'Yesterday's Child', featured original illustrations by Beatrix Potter and others. Potter's illustrations are the centerpiece of the collection. In one, we see Peter Rabbit having his jacket straightened by his attentive mother. The collector's notes explained the joy of collecting in terms with which we can all relate. She noted that 'my companions of years past surround me every day where they continue to delight'. The popularity of the all-too-few showings of these private collections attests to the fact that there are many of us who enjoy them too.

Private collectors of Potter's art have flourished in the United States. Two watercolors, 'Rabbit dancing to a piper' and 'Rabbits playing blindman's buff', are privately owned, having been given to Henry P. Coolidge, the son of a friend, by Potter herself. Reproductions of these drawings, which were originally part of a set of six, were available to the general public.

Potter also has her celebrity American fans. The famed children's author Maurice Sendak is another well-known collector, and it has been rumored that Rose Kennedy bought original Potter illustrations for her children. *The Horn Book* Company owns several letters from Potter to Bertha Mahoney, a *Horn Book* editor who developed a long and close relationship with Potter. Potter also donated watercolor illustrations to Boston's Bookshop for Boys and Girls, the original home of *The Horn Book*. For their seventy-fifth

Maurice Sendak, writer and illustrator of children's books, in the porch at Hill Top

49

anniversary, *The Horn Book* paid tribute to Potter by putting the Potter letters and the watercolors in their virtual exhibition. They also used an illustration as part of their anniversary issue and produced posters of the front cover as well.

While the interest in private collection has increased the value of Potter's art, it has had sometimes a negative effect on the ability of the public to see the materials. While intrepid collecting has brought much of the artwork associated with Beatrix Potter to the United States, it has also meant that it has become separated and dispersed among the many individual collectors. It is wonderful to know that there are so many enthusiastic Potter fans, but this also means that much of this artwork is not readily available for general viewing or studying.

To truly understand the huge popularity of Beatrix Potter's art in the United States, it is important to consider as the final pieces of the jigsaw, the many ways in which her art has been adapted for use in the popular media quite apart from the little books. Because the stories of Beatrix Potter retain their appeal beyond any age limit, new formats - from comic strips to McDonald's 'Happy Meals' – have been used to adapt Potter's work for children of all ages.

Just as Beatrix Potter complemented her original narrative with her own illustrations, so the story of Peter Rabbit has inspired the comic book artists of today. In recent years Dark Horse Comics has published a series of graphic novels, using the work of Beatrix Potter as inspiration. Graphic novels are similar to comic books in that each page has multiple frames with illustrations and dialogue; however, graphic novels generally offer a complete story in one book. Bryan Talbot's *The Tale of One Bad Rat* was published in the United States in four separate books by Dark Horse Comics. In this story, a runaway girl who has been sexually abused by her father finds comfort in the works of Beatrix Potter. Popular with teenagers, this series is not a re-working of any of Potter's actual books but an intriguing way to incorporate them into a completely new genre to deal with more contemporary themes.

Adult fans of Beatrix Potter have discovered even more ways to view the art from her books, as printers become ever more creative in offering reproductions for sale. In 1995, Battledore Ltd. of Kingston, New York, offered a limited edition portfolio of art prints made from her original line-blocks for *The Tale of Peter Rabbit,* for approximately $800 each. This special printing was accompanied by an introduction by Maurice Sendak, who wrote of the drawings, 'These first black and whites have much to tell us. They are nervous and jittery and full of life. There is a skittishness and a dash that – alas – could never be preserved in the polished edition with illustrations that have been embellished and perfected'.

Even when we look at the illustrations themselves, we see that the publishing

50

world has found new ways to retell *The Tale of Peter Rabbit* by incorporating Potter's designs into a variety of different media. Videos depicting the story of Peter Rabbit, often produced in England, are very popular with American children and can be found in almost any American public library, alongside the books that inspired them. An interactive CD Rom entitled 'The Adventures of Peter Rabbit & Benjamin Bunny' has also been developed by Mindscape; this allows children to navigate from one scene to the next in two animated stories and six activity areas. Other software, 'Peter Rabbit's Math Garden', teaches basic arithmetic to young children.

It is no surprise that other industries have taken an interest in using Beatrix Potter's storybook illustrations for a variety of American products. Wild Apple Graphics of Vermont acquired an exclusive license to print and sell posters of Beatrix Potter's famous animal characters in North America. Happily, the president of Wild Apple Graphics, John Chester, is committed to maintaining the integrity of Potter's art. Other well-known American companies have applied Potter's characters to stationery and for decorative purposes. Hallmark Cards is among those marketing Potter's work. In 1997 Motif Designs chose Beatrix Potter's art for a new line of textiles for home decorating. 'The World of Beatrix Potter' includes seven borders and wallpapers and four new fabrics. Improvements in printing technology allow the illustrations of Potter's books to be faithfully recreated on these unfamiliar materials.

Beatrix Potter's art is seen as a wonderful way to grab the attention of the consumer and sell a variety of products in the United States. But that may be a use that was beyond the intention of Peter Rabbit's creator. It is interesting to note that in one of the letters from Potter to *The Horn Book* editor Bertha Mahony, she writes, 'I do hate anything like advertisement'. Who knows if fifty years would have changed her mind, but it certainly appears that the advertising world loves Beatrix Potter.

'This Season @ Hudson's', a department store catalog published in the spring of 1998, celebrated Potter's art with an illustration on its front cover and a story about her life. While the catalog featured plush bunnies, stationery, candies and other items for sale, the sketch that was chosen for the cover is not from one of Potter's many books, but a scientific illustration. As part of its month-long promotion, every Hudson's store had a special gift shop filled with exclusive Beatrix Potter merchandise. Even McDonald's Restaurant, producer of the quintessentially American hamburger, has used Beatrix Potter's artwork to sell its products. In 1988 the children's 'Happy Meal' was sold with a Beatrix Potter storybook. The burger, French fries, drink and book were packaged in a box covered with Potter's illustrations. Children were given the opportunity to

One of the Teleflora Easter displays featuring
a scene from *The Tale of Peter Rabbit* on
a themed vase

navigate a maze (to help Peter find his way home), learn jokes about rabbits and gardening facts, and connect the dots to reveal a picture of Squirrel Nutkin.

For the past few years, 'Peter Rabbit and Friends' has been the theme of Easter celebrations at my local shopping mall, WestFarms in Farmington, Connecticut. In Center Court there are animated decorations including Peter Rabbit jumping out of a watering can. As part of the celebration, children and adults can have Breakfast with Peter Rabbit and children are invited to have their photo taken with Peter Rabbit himself! This was a fundraising event for the Capitol Region Library Council to which my library belongs. Another form of advertising is used by Teleflora, a national floral distributor in the United States. For several years, live flower arrangements have been created in Peter Rabbit themed vases for the Easter season.

Beatrix Potter is now such a well-recognized reference point in American popular culture that her work has even provided the situations for cartoons drawn by her fans. America's *New Yorker* magazine, in particular, is well-known for its witty sense of humor. In recent years, a couple of the cartoons featured in the magazine that contain references to Beatrix Potter's work have been brought to my attention.

In one, the artist pokes fun at American attorneys. Peter Rabbit is on the witness stand and the attorney is asking him to 'please stand and point to the person you know as Mr McGregor', while Mr McGregor sits at the defendant's table. A legal dispute between Peter and Mr McGregor was also the subject of cartoons written and illustrated by the late Charles M. Schulz for his internationally syndicated Peanuts comic strip. Surely, it is a sign of the extensive influence of Beatrix Potter's work that these characters are now instantly recognizable and a part of American popular culture.

Throughout the United States there is much evidence that the popularity of Peter Rabbit and the art of Beatrix Potter continue to endure – from libraries to museums to web sites to even the funnies in the newspaper. Many years after other children's authors have been forgotten, interest in this unique and talented artist is undiminished. Furthermore, the jigsaw puzzle of exhibitions, private collections and popular media has brought Potter's art to even greater numbers of Americans during the last twenty years. But when we have all the pieces of the jigsaw puzzle in front of us, we should not forget what the puzzle looks like when it is completed. While Beatrix Potter's art has become disseminated throughout American popular culture, her legacy would soon mean nothing without the illustrated books that continue to delight adults and children alike. Through the continued support of the Beatrix Potter Society and those who love, collect and showcase her art, we expect that many future generations of Americans will become Beatrix Potter enthusiasts too!

"If you would, Peter, please stand and point to the person you know as Mr. McGregor."

A cartoon from the *New Yorker* magazine, indicating the wide-spread recognition of Beatrix Potter's best-known characters

Beatrix Potter and Natural History

PETER HOLLINDALE

O NCE UPON A TIME there was a lady called Beatrix Potter, who wrote charming animal stories for young children. She died in 1943, living long enough to see Hitler doomed. Three years later another Beatrix Potter was born, and her midwife was Margaret Lane. This Beatrix had lived an eccentric, repressed and lonely childhood, confined to the third floor of her unsympathetic parents' house in Bolton Gardens, London. She lived in a solitude relieved only by the companionship of her brother Bertram, six years her junior, until his departure for school condemned her to further years of isolation. The snobbery and social narrowness of her parents made her pathologically shy, so that she sought solace with the pet rabbits, hedgehogs, mice, rats, snails, lizards and other assorted creatures she was able to secrete in the nursery.

This private zoological life, both with and without Bertram, was anything but sentimental or squeamish. 'They decided to make a collection of all the plants, animals and insects they could find, and smuggled home innumerable beetles, toadstools, dead birds, hedgehogs, frogs, caterpillars, minnows, and sloughed snakeskins. If the dead specimen were not past skinning, they skinned it; if it were, they busily boiled it and kept the bones.' (Lane, 1946) This Beatrix 'made friends with rabbits and hedgehogs, mice and minnows, as a prisoner in solitary confinement will befriend a mouse'. (ibid.) For a whole decade, from the age of seventeen to twenty-seven 'she simply moved, a captive planet, through the Potter phases'. (ibid.) 'At some point in it she took up, and at another abandoned, the study of fungus.' (ibid.) Then, early in the 1890s, fragments of publication start to appear, and they lead to *The Tale of Peter Rabbit*, and the period of rather more than a decade, between the turn of the century and the First World War, when the work that really matters, the writing of the little books, was done, until in 1913 Beatrix achieved the marital independence she had so long wanted. Then she retired to her final existence as Mrs Heelis of Sawrey, whose remaining thirty years can be amply covered in twenty-seven pages.

I do not seek to denigrate Margaret Lane, who is indispensable to our gradual uncovering of the life-cycle of Beatrix Potter. On the contrary, the essential clues to Beatrix Potter the naturalist can all be found in Lane's original opening chapters. When she describes the young Beatrix hidden under the table at her grandmother's home at Camfield Place, eavesdropping on the grown-ups, and later making surreptitious coded notes as she sat up to the table, Lane is showing us Potter the student of human natural history, which is so important to our understanding of her. Lane tells us how the countryside became more real to Beatrix than the town, with an interest that embraced not only wild and farmyard animals, but 'the human scene as well'. (ibid.) She shows us the early fascination with both fact and fantasy, and the early link between science and art. She even casually mentions Rupert Potter's interest in the Lake Poets. And all this without the coded diaries to assist her. Her only serious error was to represent Potter's childhood and youth as darker, colder, lonelier than in fact they were.

Everything changed with the discovery of Potter's coded diaries, and that momentous day in 1958 when Leslie Linder broke the code. 'Working through the *Journal* word-by-word and sheet-by-sheet,' he wrote, 'it was strange how one forgot about Beatrix Potter the author of the *Peter Rabbit* books, and became conscious of a charming person called *Miss Potter,* who lived at Number Two, Bolton Gardens, London'. (Potter, *Journal* 1966, xxvi.) Suddenly the world knew hugely more about Miss Potter from the age of fourteen onwards. There was no longer a shy, dim, tedious, blank decade of early womanhood, and Margaret Lane's picture had to be re-drawn. She redrew it herself, a little grudgingly I think, in 1978.

Over the last twenty years, since the foundation of the Beatrix Potter Society, the process has accelerated enormously. The thirty-year life of Mrs Heelis of Sawrey is no longer just an unexpected happy coda to nearly fifty years of family repression, but has interest in its own right – for many reasons, but chiefly because the formidable Mrs Heelis was a pioneering landscape conservationist and an expert on Herdwick sheep. Likewise those early years of solitude in the nursery have been looked at again. Rupert and Helen Potter may not be everyone's idea of model parents, but Rupert in particular has improved considerably on mature acquaintance, and his own tastes, talents and activities can be given due credit for the fact that his daughter's art became so much more than conventional feminine accomplishment.

Moreover, if we so choose, we can draw up a considerable roll-call of significant figures in the life of Beatrix Potter: Rupert Potter, Bertram Potter, Mr

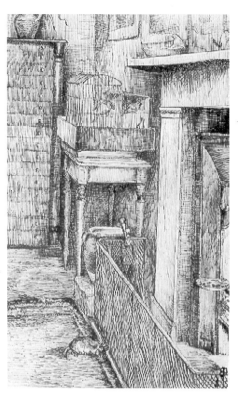

Gaskell, John Bright, Sir John Millais, Sir Henry Roscoe, Charlie McIntosh, Norman Warne, Hardwicke Rawnsley, William Heelis, Tom Storey. This was a lady who was really quite fortunate, or astute, or both, in finding a man for all seasons.

How much we know, nowadays. The life-cycle of Beatrix Potter is like a human version of the butterfly's: egg, caterpillar, chrysalis, imago. 'What, you egg!' says the murderer to Macduff's son, as might those in authority have said to the egg Beatrix if they had discovered the full extent of the menagerie, abattoir and pathology lab at Bolton Gardens. Those years of relative seclusion with the pets and corpses were the making of a naturalist, in part; but another part, parentally encouraged, was the painstaking apprenticeship in art: the drawing and copying, the visits to art galleries, the sustained precocious art criticism, and also the regular excursions to the Natural History Museum – the incessant self-teaching as artist, natural scientist and acute observer. What we are now well placed to see is the sheer *professionalism* of it all, starting at so young an age. As Anne Stevenson Hobbs writes in *A Victorian Naturalist*:

A pen-and-ink sketch showing a corner of the schoolroom at No. 2 Bolton Gardens, done in 1885. In the background is a specimen cabinet for Beatrix and Bertram's natural history collections

> Science goes hand in hand with imagination in Beatrix Potter's earliest art. Already a serious naturalist at the age of nine, she recorded in her own words the feeding habits of caterpillars; in her journal she speculated on the comparative evolution of fossils and fungi. Later, and sometimes for publication, she made more formal notes; her writings are vividly visual, notably in 'A Walk Amongst the Funguses'. Thoroughly professional in her science, she aimed at analysis and accuracy.

To see how far we have come in our knowledge and valuation of her work during the last twenty years, take this extract from Lynn Barber's *The Heyday of*

Natural History 1820-1870, published in 1980. It comes in a chapter on 'Victorian lady naturalists':

> Victorian women rarely translated their genuine enthusiasm for natural history into any purposeful form of research . . .. Illustration was the only form of natural history work in which women really excelled. Marianne North's oil paintings of flowers in the Kew Museum, or Anne Pratt's illustrations of ferns and wild flowers, or Mrs William Buckland's drawings of fossils, or even [even!] the young Beatrix Potter's studies of mushrooms can all stand comparison with any male work.

The mycology is not my direct concern in this talk: I hope to set Potter's natural history in a broader context. And of course we know that Barber's patronising comment here had already been rendered obsolete by Dr W.P.K. Findlay's use of Potter's drawings for *Wayside and Woodland Fungi* in 1967. But it shows a residual attitude which has changed noticeably in the last few years. Potter, however special a case, was part of a wider movement which was changing the scientific artwork of gifted women from a social asset to a professional skill. Anne Hobbs describes the change:

> By 1800, flower painting had become a required female accomplishment, and a harmless antidote to frivolity. Sketching was proper and universal; watercolours, being small-scale and clean, were especially recommended to young ladies. By mid-century, thanks largely to Ruskin's influence, art was being systematically taught even to women and often *by* women. Many women became distinguished botanical artists, and some of these women worked as professionals.

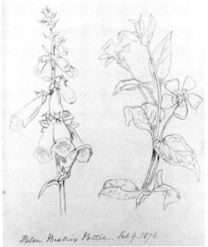

'Foxglove and Periwinkle': an early sketch signed 'Helen Beatrix Potter' and dated 1876

Nevertheless, it was the artwork which took precedence in women's lives. When Beatrix *did* engage in a 'purposeful form of research', even the prestigious support of her uncle, Sir Henry Roscoe, could not help her to overcome the barrier of scientific conservatism. In those years of the late 1880s and the 1890s a second Beatrix Potter, one who had developed from the youthful eclectic natural historian and artist into a potential research scientist, a scientific illustrator, and a mycologist of distinction, appeared and was suppressed. So the second important stage of the life-cycle gave way to the third and most famous, that of the children's author, motivated by the need for independence, economic and otherwise. The need for this Beatrix Potter ceased, except for fitful and half-hearted reappearances, when she became Mrs Heelis of Sawrey. She herself would undoubtedly have seen those thirty Lakeland years as the 'imago' period of her life. The world at large re-draws the sequence and sees her most complete self in the books. Scientists perhaps see it in the achievements and the might-have-beens of her mycology. At least the evidence is now there, and the total achievement properly catalogued and documented in the Linder Collection and the Armitt Collection, and in published studies.

What is quite clear is that Potter had an astonishing capacity to re-invent herself, in response to circumstances and her own ambitions, as her life went on. She was adaptable, inventive, enterprising, versatile, yet also in many respects conservative and dutiful. But there are common denominators running through the whole course of her life, and one of these is that there is no time, from early childhood to old age, when she was not concerned with creatures other than the human, beginning with nursery pets and ending with Herdwick sheep. Equally, however, it is clear from her diaries and letters that there was no phase of her life when animals *replaced* the human in her interests. Despite her personal shyness, the species which interested her always included the human species, an interest not subdued either by the solitude of the nursery or the privacy of Castle Cottage.

I would want to add three other general observations, all of them germane I think to our understanding of her as a natural scientist. First, that she is always alert to both fact and fantasy about the creatures she observes, and never mixes the two up except with conscious intent. Second, that she makes no distinction of interest between wild and domestic animals, though she is sharply alert to the differences, as between wild and domestic rabbits. She enjoys the boundary line between wild and tame. Look for instance at her marvellous *Journal* entry for 28 March 1885 about cats, which begins 'There are signs that the domestic animals are revolting'. And note the carefully two-sided name 'John Stoat Ferret' in *The Tale of Mr Tod*. Third, that in the animals she studies she is always aware of both the individual and the species – noticing for instance that even snails are not identical in their behaviour. Her concern with both individual and species applies just as much to the human animal as to any other. These are the building blocks from which Potter's natural history is made, and they account for the wonderful elasticity and variousness of outlook which made her both scientific observer and imaginative artist, and sometimes both at once.

Using these building blocks, then, I want to step back from the detailed studies of recent years and ask what *kind* of natural historian Potter was. In her work on mycology, so disappointingly cut short, she was obviously the product of a new scientific age. Much of her less specialised work shows the same modernity of outlook, the same meticulous concern for factual evidence: the culture of the microscope. But she also draws, consciously or not, on older traditions and influences, all of them feeding that many-sided outlook which made her so adaptable, and so hard to classify.

As an example, I would like to illustrate her line of descent from one of the greatest of all amateur naturalists, Gilbert White, whose *Natural History and Antiquities of Selborne* (1788) is a classic work. In this passage we can see White, an eighteenth-century clergyman, exemplifying the naturalist's crucial gift: intelligent questioning and inference, based on careful, accurate observation. He is examining the wheat-ball nest of a harvest mouse:

> As this nest was perfectly full, how could the dam come at her litter respectively so as to administer a teat to each? perhaps she opens different places for that purpose, adjusting them again when the business is over: but she could not possibly be contained herself in the ball with her young, which moreover would be daily increasing in bulk. This wonderful procreant cradle, an elegant instance of the efforts of instinct, was found in a wheat-field, suspended in the head of a thistle.

The scientist here is also versed in literature: notice the integral Shakespearean quotation, 'procreant cradle', such as we find many times in the *Journal*. But the habitual intelligent use of observation is what matters. I take just three small examples from Potter's visit to Cornwall in 1892. Her account of that visit in the *Journal* generally illustrates another tradition she inherits, which I will turn to in a moment, but here are three characteristic details:

> That the soil is not so good as it looks, I judged decidedly from the great numbers of rooks.
> We only saw one hawk, a sparrow hawk, during this long expedition. They seem singularly scarce, and perhaps for that reason, little birds are proportionally numerous.
> . . . the beach in parts is literally composed of shells. Their variety is doubtless due to the warm sea.

The *Journal* is full of similar observations. Like White, she notices things, records them, and uses them as the starting-point for theories. That is the way a good naturalist's mind works. Even when she was wrong, as she was for example about the potentially adverse effects of sparrowhawks on populations of small birds, her speculations are always thoughtful and intelligent.

There is also the human side. Here is Gilbert White, observing his aunt's pet tortoise:

I was much taken with its sagacity in discerning those that do it kind offices; for as soon as the good old lady comes in sight who has waited on it for more than thirty years, it hobbles towards its benefactress with awkward alacrity; but remains inattentive to strangers. Thus not only *'the ox knoweth his owner, and the ass his master's crib'*, but the most abject reptile and torpid of beings distinguishes the hand that feeds it, and is touched with the feelings of gratitude!

In this case there is no need to cite particular equivalents in Potter. With a similar blend of affectionate observation and playful amusement she projects human feelings and motives on to her pets, but both she and White are just as interested in the animal behaviour, the 'otherness', of the creatures they are watching. This double view, this ability to humanise playfully, while avoiding sentimentality and self-deception, is essential to Potter's eventual triumph in the little books.

Perceiving the animals as if they were human, however frowned upon by scientists, is a naturalist's pleasure, and both White and Potter enjoyed it. Arguably more important still is the gift of perceiving humans as animals – not just by metaphor or caricature, not simply as in fable and folktale, revealing as these are, but as animals in reality. Before political correctness intervened, the naturalist's eye was unashamedly first caught by deformity, whether mental or physical. (And the poet's eye, too, as in Wordsworth's contribution to *Lyrical Ballads*.) Here is White, the naturalist at work on human nature:

> We had in this village more than twenty years ago an idiot-boy, whom I well remember, who, from a child, showed a strong propensity to bees; they were his food, his amusement, his sole object . . .. Honey-bees, humble-bees, and wasps, were his prey wherever he found them: he had no apprehensions from their stings, but would seize them *nudis manibus,* and at once disarm them of their weapons, and suck their bodies for the sake of their honey-bags . . .. He was a very *merops apiaster,* or bee-bird; and very injurious to men that kept bees; for he would slide into their bee-gardens, and, sitting down before the stools, would rap with his finger on the hives, and so take the bees as they came out . . .. As he ran about he used to make a humming noise with his lips, resembling the buzzing of bees.

Potter too had an eye for human singularities. She found some in Ambleside in 1886. 'Extraordinary number of local curiosities. Old gentleman, blue on one side of his face, boy without a nose, extremely bandy retriever of Dr Redmayne, lady lodger with a black moustache, idiot, and Town Crier.' (*Journal.*) White and Potter were only human, and no doubt part of their fascination was the same that draws customers to freak shows; but another part is truly natural history, the urge to record intriguing variants on the human species, and departures from behavioural norms. Potter's *Journal* is full of cameos of people

60

she has seen, met or heard of, who are physically or mentally unusual. She is not being voyeuristic or heartless, and indeed she directs the same sharp eye at many so-called 'normal' people, including her own family. Nowadays books such as Desmond Morris's *The Human Animal: A Personal View of the Human Species* do the same thing on a larger scale. For the naturalist, nature includes human nature. Gilbert White knew that, and Potter's *Journal* lies in the same tradition.

I think it is impossible to over-emphasise this aspect of Potter's natural history, or to explain the uniqueness of the little books without it. One of the finest achievements in post-war published natural history has been the Collins 'New Naturalist' series, which includes an excellent volume by H.J. Fleure called *A Natural History of Man in Britain*, subtitled 'Conceived as a study of changing relations between Men and Environment'. Even modern readers are sometimes surprised to find themselves regarded as a topic for natural history, but it would not have surprised or disconcerted Potter. The editors say in their introduction that the book, a serious academic work, 'will bring the reader no nearer to deciding whether Professor Fleure is an historian, anthropologist, geographer or naturalist, so perfectly does he combine the varied approaches'. In the *Journal*, quite informally, Potter too is both historian, anthropologist, geographer and naturalist. She too has an inter-disciplinary mind. All four of those approaches are present, for instance, in this paragraph from her *Journal* record of her visit to Cornwall in 1892:

> The people here are all singularly alike, and one can well believe the statement that they are the purest bred race in Britain. I am only surprised that the old Cornish dialect has died out earlier than several others, for they are extremely isolated in situation, and if one or two persons whom I have talked to were fair examples, they are naive and unspoiled to an amusing degree. Very friendly, kindly, cheerful, healthy, long-lived, and the numerous old people very merry, which speaks well for a race.

She goes on in visual terms to anatomise their physical characteristics with just the same kind of intellectual interest that she brought to articulating a fox's skeleton. In effect she is describing the sub-species or race of an animal, in relation to its history and environment, and there is a lovely moment when she has to record an individual failure of her classifying system: 'Our driver has a head like a dagger (he was particularly Cornish, very civil, but with a certain naive dignity or reserve. I was shocked to discover that this man was Scotch)'.

Potter is anticipating Fleure's natural science of humankind, as it appeared seventy years later, but she is also inheriting and furthering an older tradition, to which I think the origins of Fleure's science can be traced. She is the detached and sharp-eyed travelling observer, and passages like this in her *Journal* have

61

their sources in, say, Defoe's *Tour Through the Whole Island of Great Britain*, in the writings of Celia Fiennes, in the journal of Fanny Burney (clearly a favourite book of Beatrix's), and in William Cobbett's *Rural Rides*. All those extensive Potter family holidays emerge in the *Journal* as a mixture of human and non-human natural history, and in her *Journal* we can see that double interest growing into what became a branch of modern natural science. By noting her eclectic inter-disciplinary scientific interests, we can also place her in a literary tradition.

Living when she did, as an educated late nineteenth-century reader, she was inevitably in part a post-Romantic, carrying in her mind the influences of the English Romantic poets, as well as contemporaries like Ruskin. Understanding of nature in this period is inseparable from the appreciation of landscapes. As a painter, Potter was of course a distinguished miniaturist, her art and science meeting in the microscope's revelation of detail. But she also painted landscapes, and many of the illustrations to the little books are placed against realistic back-grounds, often still there to be seen. My purpose is to show how many strands there were in her broad-based intelligence – her sheer eclecticism – and the diverse influences that affected it. One of these was certainly Wordsworth.

On her visit to Keswick in 1885, she wrote in the *Journal* about the drownings that resulted from the drunken misadventures of the town's roughs. These miscreants were in a boat returning at dusk from an alcoholic binge at the Lodore Hotel:

> Those drowned were John Gill, Thomas Lightfoot, and Harry Mitchell. They belonged to the lowest set in the town, and will not be missed, but unfortunately the catastrophe has had no effect on the survivors, they were fighting in Keswick within an hour after. They and all the roughs and idle in the place have been dragging day and night since, the weather being fortunately calm, and the moon growing to the full . . ..
> They also dived – but on Saturday night, two boys who thought they would have a try, brought up a body at the first drag. It came up like a cork, caught by the flaps of the coat . . ... It is most horrible having those things under the water, we hardly like to go up the lake.

This ghastly tale of figures in a landscape, the human grotesque among natural beauty at Derwentwater, strongly recalls the young Wordsworth at Esthwaite, as he tells in Book 5 of *The Prelude*:

> While I was roving up and down alone,
> Seeking I knew not what, I chanced to cross
> One of those open fields, which, shaped like ears,
> Make green peninsulas on Esthwaite's Lake:
> Twilight was coming on, yet through the gloom

Appeared distinctly on the opposite shore
A heap of garments, as if left by one
Who might have there been bathing. Long I watched,
But no one owned them; meanwhile the calm lake
Grew dark with all the shadows on its breast,
And, now and then, a fish up-leaping snapped
The breathless stillness. The succeeding day,
Those unclaimed garments telling a plain tale
Drew to the spot an anxious crowd; some looked
In passive expectation from the shore,
While from a boat others hung o'er the deep,
Sounding with grappling irons and long poles.
At last, the dead man, 'mid that beauteous scene
Of trees and hills and water, bolt upright
Rose, with his ghastly face, a spectre shape
Of terror . . .

Potter goes on from her account of the drownings straight to a passage of
verbal landscape drawing which is utterly Wordsworthian in tone. Remember
Wordsworth's 'the stars / Eastward were sparkling clear, and in the west / The

A watercolour impression of
Derwentwater from the 1903
Derwentwater Sketchbook, now the property
of the National Trust

orange sky of evening died away', (Wordsworth 1850, Book I) or 'It is a beauteous evening, calm and free / The holy time is quiet as a Nun / Breathless with adoration', (Wordsworth, sonnet 1807) and then listen to Potter, after she has told her sorry tale:

> When this happened it was a most lovely evening, warm and sultry, not a breeze of wind. The sunset was still fiery in the west and south, the moon was rising, the reflections of the great blue mountains lay broad and motionless in the water, undisturbed save now and then by the ripple of a passing boat. East, south and north, the blue mountains with their crimson crests towered up against a clear blue heaven, flecked with little white fleecy clouds. Westward the thunder clouds came rolling across the fire; yet under such a sky, and amidst such peace and calm, one hears shouting and drunken voices singing.

The loveliness of nature, coupled with the physical blemish of man-in-nature, are beautifully caught in Potter's late-Romantic, post-Wordsworthian writing here, reflecting another formative influence on her thinking. The pictures for the little books are gentler versions of her sensibility to figures in a landscape.

I come now to one of the enigmas in Potter's thinking about natural history. Somewhere in her pages, perhaps, there are answers to it, but I have not come across them. Instead I am left with one fascinating but elusive passage in the *Journal*. No one can doubt what was the nineteenth century's most significant event for the natural scientist. It was the publication in 1859 of Darwin's great theory of evolution, *On the Origin of Species by Means of Natural Selection*. One of Darwin's supporters was Thomas Henry Huxley, who published *Man's Place in Nature* in 1863. Inhabiting the intellectual milieu that she did, it is impossible that Potter as a young adult was uninformed about these major, controversial works, with their direct bearing on her own interests as an analytical student of natural history. Yet I can find only two references to Darwin in the *Journal*, and only one of consequence. This one seems to me very revealing, though I deal with it only tentatively.

In 1894 Potter went to stay with her cousin, Caroline Hutton, at Harescombe Grange, Stroud. Even without other evidence, it is clear from Potter's account what kind of person Caroline was: she was brilliant, educated, in love with ideas, intellectually fearless and uncompromising. That is one way of describing her. In her *Journal* Potter had another, shorter way: 'Caroline is a pickle'. She clearly meant much to Beatrix from the first. In the holiday at Lennel later in 1894, she says she is 'very much vexed that I could not have the Hutton girls', and then, wistfully, 'I would so very much have liked to have Caroline'. From Caroline she would have hoped for scientific aid as well as companionship.

At Stroud it is fairly clear that Caroline was not only a pickle but a Darwinian.

Potter's response to her performance, in the midst of her less advanced family, tells us a lot:

> Mary [Caroline's sister] who seems to be curious to discover whether I should be shocked with so much Huxley and Darwin, told me confidentially that Lady Lingen was the only person who had any influence with Caroline. I was once or twice shocked with that young person; at other times I thought her perfect. The prevailing impression was of freshness and extreme amusement. The keynote of her character is decision and complete absence of imagination. There results therefore an almost idolatry of truth, and knowledge which is truth. She cannot understand that there is such a thing as 'letting well alone', or that, as Mary plaintively put it, 'whatever Caroline may say, there are some things that nobody can understand!'

Potter seems to have remonstrated with Caroline about the effect of her uncompromising views on those less able than herself:

> I brought tears into her eyes when I spoke about poor Annie Coldrick, the girl they are so kind to, who is dying of consumption. I suggested that though Huxley was sufficient for an educated person like Caroline, it would be a poor exchange and indeed an impossible creed for the lower classes.

Caroline protests that she would not dream of unsettling Annie Coldrick, but Potter says 'I was thinking of Mary too, and certain slight disrespect to Mrs Hutton, but truth is truth'.

What did Potter mean by 'truth is truth'? There are shades here of Richard Dawkins's uncompromising, militant Darwinian atheism in our own time, which may be an exhilarating truth for him but not, perhaps, for Everyman. That, at any rate, seems to have been Potter's view. 'Truth is truth' may be a critical snapshot of Caroline's stubborn intellectual integrity, with no complicity on Potter's part. Or it may be a guarded concession of agreement, offset by compunction about wrecking the beliefs of others. Either way, she clearly felt such compunction. For Potter there was more to life than intellectual rigour, even about such a massive idea as evolution.

My own feeling is that Potter was not much concerned with large theories, even of natural history. I think she was above all an empirical observer, a taxonomist and an analyst, fascinated by the What? How? and Why? of immediate natural phenomena. Her vocation was to investigate a crowded universe of small things. I suspect that she gave to Caroline, and through her to Darwin and Huxley, a half-committed agreement, while not believing that evolution or any other theory accounted for everything. That is why she accuses Caroline of 'complete absence of imagination', and notes that 'with all her cleverness she could not understand why I enjoyed the service in Gloucester Cathedral'. I suspect too that she never chose or needed to go far beyond her *Journal* entry for 30 September 1884, where she observes that 'All outward forms of religion are almost useless, and are the cause of endless strife. What do Creeds matter? Believe there is a great power silently working all things for good, behave yourself and never mind the rest'.

Much study of Potter in recent years has concentrated on her artwork, and quite rightly so. Now that her mycology has been duly recognised, Potter the scientific observer has been added to Potter the children's artist. My argument has been that in order to understand her natural history completely (and incidentally the little books as well) we must spread the net more widely. This means paying as much attention to what she wrote as to what she drew, especially to the *Journal*, and firmly including human natural history as an intrinsic part of her intellectual repertoire. The *Journal* shows her to possess a high-spirited intellect, fully engaged in the current themes of her age, and as a highly educated reader who drew knowingly on some literary influences and was the unconscious legatee of others. Add to that the eventual practicalities of farming, and you have a many-sided outlook.

The observer is certainly interesting enough. For instance, in the spring of 1883 she records her observation of London birds, noting that she has seen cock-robins fighting, 'but usually only one cock-red-breast, never see a hen'. She evidently did not know that male and female robins are virtually identical, both having red breasts. But how astute she was generally, in the days before field guides, when self-help was the only option.

Mr McGregor puzzles over the rabbit footmarks

Observation, though, is never the whole story. There is also fantasy, and anthropomorphic wit. This was the quality that turned robins into Mr McGregor's security guards in *The Tale of Peter Rabbit* and *The Tale of Benjamin Bunny*. In one delightful illustration of *Benjamin Bunny* on page 57, as Mr McGregor puzzles over the rabbit footmarks in his garden, the cat who has fallen down on the job of guarding his domain rubs

Peter and Benjamin dash into their newly excavated burrow, from *The Tale of Mr Tod*

smarmily against his legs, while his other ally, the robin, is a tiny watchful presence in the distance.

Fact and fantasy are often wittily co-existent in the stories. Rabbits in the *Journal* are both characters and 'regular vermin'. In *The Tale of Mr Tod*, when Peter and Benjamin seek refuge down the rabbit hole they have excavated at Bull Banks, they are 'foolish' considered as persons, but as rabbits are behaving with natural instinct. Pigling Bland and Alexander set off for market, destined humanly for gainful employment, and piggily for bacon. Drawing on several traditions, and several kinds of personal experience, Beatrix Potter's natural history makes room for many different responses to her world. Let me illustrate this from one particular example, the badger, and show it spread over her lifetime.

Here is Potter with Caroline Hutton at Stroud in 1894, very much the field naturalist:

> I was extremely interested with the badger's marks and their claw-walks, worn bare and slippery underneath the nettles and brush, but could judge they were made by a large stumpy animal, and the size of their footsteps is quite startling in an English wood . . . we saw their tracks in a lane half a mile from the Earths. The latter are curious, struck out by the hind legs like a rabbit's hole, but a square piled-up bank like the spoil-banks in front of a coalpit.

Some years later, in *The Tale of Mr Tod*, she depicts Tommy Brock as a disagreeable animal, of dirty and unpleasant habits. She maligns the badger outrageously. In 'Aesop in the Shadows' I suggest some possible reasons why, but the one I favour is that the badger was humanised in that story to embody her sense of proletarian threat in the English society of her time.

Many years afterwards, in old age, there is a different response again, this time recording her affection for literature's most famous badger, in Kenneth Grahame's *The Wind in the Willows*. She likes him partly because (unlike Toad) he does not 'fly in the face of nature':

> at least all writers for children ought to have a sufficient recognition of what things look like – did he not describe 'Toad' as combing his *hair*? A mistake to fly in the face of nature . . .. So I prefer Badger. (Potter, *Letters*, 1989.)

As for real badgers, W.R. Mitchell in his *Beatrix Potter Remembered* records an interview with Anthony Benson from Troutbeck Farm, of Potter's Lakeland days:

> When Anthony killed a badger, he thought he had done a good thing. Mrs Heelis got to know about it and she asked why he had slain the badger. I said: 'Well, a badger worries lambs and things like that'. She said: 'Oh, no it doesn't.' I nearly got my notice over that badger. She was reet upset.

The life-cycle of a naturalist, from egg to imago, from young Beatrix in the nursery to Mrs Heelis: none of its phases is dispensable. Like the badger, many interests appear and reappear in different guises. Across her life we see the field naturalist, the artist, the pet-lover, the pathologist, the research mycologist, the anthropomorphic storyteller, the student of the human animal, the cultured reader, the post-Romantic devotee of landscapes, the practical farmer, the conservationist: all play their parts in the complex phenomenon of Beatrix Potter, natural historian.

REFERENCES

Barber, Lynn, *The Heyday of Natural History 1820-1870*, Cape, 1980
Cobbett, William, *Rural Rides*, 1830 (many editions)
Darwin, Charles, *On the Origin of Species by Means of Natural Selection*, 1859 (many editions)
Defoe, Daniel, *Tour through the Whole Island of Great Britain*, 1724-6 (many editions)
Fiennes, Celia, *The Journeys of Celia Fiennes*, Cresset Press, 1947
Findlay, W.P.K., *Wayside and Woodland Fungi*, Warne, 1967
*Fleure, H.J., *A Natural History of Man in Britain*, Collins, 1951
*Hobbs, Anne Stevenson, 'Beatrix Potter's Scientific Art', in Jay, E., Noble, M., and Hobbs, A.S., (eds.), *A Victorian Naturalist: Beatrix Potter's Drawings from the Armitt Collection*, Warne, 1992
Huxley, T.H., *Man's Place in Nature*, 1863
*Lane, Margaret, *The Tale of Beatrix Potter*, Warne, 1946
Lane, Margaret, *The Magic Years of Beatrix Potter*, Warne, 1978.
*Mitchell, W.R., *Beatrix Potter Remembered,* Dalesman Books, 1987
Morris, Desmond, *The Human Animal: A Personal View of the Human Species*, BBC Books, 1994
*Potter, Beatrix, *The Journal of Beatrix Potter from 1881 to 1897*. Transcribed from her code writing by Leslie Linder, Warne, 1966, new edition, 1989.
*Potter, Beatrix, *Beatrix Potter's Letters*, ed. Judy Taylor, Warne, 1989
*White, Gilbert, *The Natural History and Antiquities of Selborne*, 1788; Dent, Everyman edition, 1949
*Wordsworth, William, *The Prelude*, 1850 (many editions)

Items asterisked are quoted in the text.

Mischievous mushrooms: Beatrix Potter's affair with fungi – facts and misunderstandings

ROY WATLING

B EATRIX POTTER illustrated over 250 species of fungi in more than 335 watercolours, some of which are now in the Perth Museum and Art Gallery, Scotland, and in the Victoria and Albert Museum, London, but most of which are in the Armitt Library, Ambleside. There may be even more, judging from relatively recent auction details and the odd discovery in private collections. Some are duplicates, with copies in the Armitt Library and the originals in Perth, the latter having been sent to Charles McIntosh. A viewing of the originals, in four folios, in 1986 and again in 1992, allowed me to ascertain the potential of these illustrations as early records of fungi. Further analysis was undoubtedly eased when John Gavin had all the illustrations photographed, so allowing work to continue without damage to the originals. It was instructive to work with these photographs over a longer period in Edinburgh, when they were left for critical review in order to produce an inventory. I must emphasise that it was only through the enthusiasm and encouragement of Dr Mary Noble that I undertook the task. It was Mary Noble, who, whilst researching for a paper, 'rediscovered' in 1984 letters sent from Beatrix Potter to the naturalist Charles McIntosh (Noble, 1985). These were obviously used as material by Coates for his book entitled *A Perthshire Naturalist* (1923). They are now deposited in the National Library of Scotland, Edinburgh. I took up the challenge to identify the fungi and I am glad that I did, as much has since unfolded. In the past fifteen years the scientific side to Beatrix's character has begun to be studied, and her work as a mycologist can now be appreciated by a wider audience.

Beatrix Potter was steeped in fairy myths, and indeed commented that 'the whole countryside belonged to the fairies'. Perhaps it was the long historic connection between fairies and fungi that first entranced her, no doubt encouraged by her Scottish nanny Mrs McKenzie, who had 'a firm belief in witches, fairies' (Taylor [etc.], 1987). Certainly the toadstools below Oatmeal Crag seemed to be fairies 'singing and bobbing and dancing in the grass' as she reported in her *Journal* in 1896. In Scotland there were many traditional stories about fungi to excite her, such as the tale of the 'Old Man of Ben Macdhui', who stumbled across a ring of beautiful dancing fairies, only for them to be changed into puffballs when he awakened from his alcoholic sleep; and of course there are always fairy rings for all to see in our parks and on our golf courses! Indeed there is a rhyme by Potter which appeared later in *A Walk with the Funguses*, a whimsical introduction especially to the boletes: 'Nid, nid, noddy, we stand in a ring, All day long, and never do a thing! But nid, nid, noddy! we wake up at night, We hop and we dance, in the merry moon-light!' 'I do not remember a time,' she reminisces, 'when I did not try to invent pictures and make fairy tales – amongst the flowers, the animals, trees, and mosses and fungi - all the thousand common objects of the countryside.' Invention, however, does not describe her treatment of archaeological, biological and geological objects over the years. Even her early attempts at painting fungi bore an excellent likeness to the real object, but after tuition from McIntosh they became scientific documents. 'The fungi raised her spirits and inspired some of the best watercolours.' (Jay [etc.], 1992.)

The first painting of a Scottish fungus by Beatrix was of 'The Old Man of the Woods', *Strobilomyces floccopus* (=*strobilaceus*). The painting was found by Mary Noble in a collection of illustrations in the possession of Mrs Joan Duke of Troutbeck, Ambleside, but Beatrix had been painting fungi before this, because there are examples dated 1888. They must have been done whilst the family were holidaying in the Lake District. Beatrix continued to illustrate fungi on her return to London after this holiday, as there are two paintings dated 'Camfield Place, December 1888', one of which depicts 'The Wood Blewit', *Lepista nuda*, a fungus which generally fruits late in the year. The illustration is an artistic rendering, but all the salient points for an accurate identification are present.

Although a further four watercolours were made in the following year, including that of the *Strobilomyces*, we have little information for the years 1890 and 1891. However, she had accrued at least a dozen or so paintings by 1892 when the family holidayed at Heath Park, Birnam, where she was able to meet Charles McIntosh. The meeting had been arranged by a mutual friend, the photographer A.F. McKenzie, although her father had been in contact with McIntosh on earlier occasions. McIntosh was a self-taught naturalist and had an

The Old Man of the Woods (*Strobilomyces floccopus*) painted at
Eastwood, Dunkeld, in 1893

excellent knowledge of the lower plants, then termed cryptogams (Coates, 1923). Beatrix described McIntosh at this Birnam meeting as 'quite painfully shy and uncouth at first, as though he was trying to swallow a muffin, and rolling his eyes about and mumbling'. He was obviously delighted to see Beatrix's paintings and commented on her accuracy. He identified some of the subjects as being rare or uncommon, while Beatrix probably only then thought from their bizarre configurations and colours that they were curiosities. Beatrix was rather a suspicious person and adds that, 'his mouth evidently watered at the chance of securing drawings'. There is no doubt that he would have been enthusiastic, having such a feel for fungi, as she comments in her *Journal*, 'When we discussed funguses he became quite excited and spoke with quite poetical feeling', and he agreed to send her fresh material for illustration. This she doubted he would do, but send material he did, and many were the subjects of her later paintings. The meeting went well, as Beatrix reciprocated with paintings, and these are now deposited in the Perth Museum and Art Gallery, along with other McIntosh memorabilia and some very important fungal specimens. Perhaps McIntosh lives on, as it is very likely that he was caricatured as Mr McGregor in *The Tale of Peter Rabbit*. (Incidentally the paintings in Perth all bear the initials CR, referring to the fact that Carleton Rea, an eminent British basidiomycetologist, had seen the paintings whilst on a foray to Blair Atholl in 1906, long after Beatrix and McIntosh had finished corresponding.)

One of the fungi McIntosh identified was a 'Saddle fungus', *Helvella crispa*,

71

illustrated from both Lingholm, Keswick, and Derwentwater, and another the 'Wood Hedgehog', *Hydnum repandum*, also illustrated from these localities. These subjects were undoubtedly contained in that original portfolio shown to McIntosh and were included in those Beatrix gifted to him. There is also a fine painting of 'The Chanterelle', *Cantharellus cibarius*, from Lingholm. We learn that McIntosh had previously found the *Helvella* by the tunnel at Inver, McIntosh's home village, and the *Hydnum* on the Murthley estate. The small discomycete *Cistella dentata*, illustrated with its germinating spores, was not painted in 1892 as indicated by some people, but executed in 1896 when Beatrix was by then studying spore development.

Correspondence exists from Rupert Potter to McIntosh, whom he must have known, if not on a personal basis, then certainly from his standing as a fine naturalist and musician. The letters detail the gift and dispatch of a copy of the Rev John Stevenson's *British Fungi – Hymenomycetes*, 1886, now in the Perth Museum and Art Gallery; this was the standard work of the day. The Rev J. Stephenson was the incumbent of Glamis and was then the Secretary of the Cryptogamic Society of Scotland and a well-established figure in British mycology (Watling, 1989). In Rupert Potter's letters, McIntosh was always referred to in the third person and this formality was continued by Beatrix in her correspondence. Two letters are known from McIntosh to Beatrix: one dated January 1894 was found in a copy of Coates's *A Perthshire Naturalist* now

Charlie McIntosh,
'The Perthshire Naturalist'

in the Armitt Library and the second, probably from 1895, was found in a geology text originally owned by Beatrix – another of her interests – and now also in the Armitt Library. Both show that the discussions which were taking place between the two were worthy of many a professional mycologist of the time, and these reinforce the high regard in which Beatrix held McIntosh: 'his judgement gave me infinitely more pleasure than that of critics who assume more and know less than poor Charlie' (*Journal*).

Probably the first fungus sent to Beatrix by McIntosh was 'The Velvet Shank', *Flammulina velutipes* (=*Agaricus velutipes*); it was painted in November 1892, reflecting its late appearance in the

72

The Velvet Shank (*Agaricus velutipes*, now *Flammulina velutipes*), painted in November 1892

year. Little did she know that she would figure this again, and indeed we now know that the spores of this fungus were the subject of the paper presented to the Linnean Society just over four years later.

In 1893, the Potters holidayed at Eastwood, near Dunkeld, on the opposite side of the Tay from the Birnam Oak, and in 1894 they were at Lennel, near Coldstream. The summers of 1895 and 1896 were spent in the Lake District. It was during these years that she was at the height of her activity. The period leading up to the presentation of her paper was therefore her most productive, as at least 172 watercolour paintings were executed. She was now in full swing! It was at Eastwood that Beatrix depicted nearly seventy fungi, including a fresh collection of *Strobilomyces floccopus*, which by then she knew was a rare fungus. It was found growing in the grounds of Eastwood and because of its particular interest she made a map of its location; this is to be found on the back of her painting of the fungus now in Perth and is dated 3 September 1893, that is one day before Beatrix in a picture-letter to Noel Moore launched Peter Rabbit. Unfortunately the grounds have been relandscaped since her time, and although a group interested in Potter and fungi found some of the features shown on the map, the fungus itself has not so far been found. Judging from the fungi still there, for example *Phylloporus pelleteri,* which are representatives of a well established mycota, it could still be present and might fruit under favourable

73

conditions. The fungus is locally common in the Severn Valley, and in Scotland in the vicinity of the valleys of the Tay and Tummel, in Black Spout Wood at Pitlochry, and at Faskally and Killiecrankie, while the specimen she painted earlier was undoubtedly from Crieff. It is also known from Darnaway (personal communication C. Miller). The early illustration dated '11.8.89' depicts a rather dried collection, probably because it had been on show at the Cryptogamic Society meeting which had been held at Crieff. How Beatrix obtained it we will never know, but at that time Francis Drummond Hay was the President of the Society and there is a suggestion that he knew about Beatrix's interest in fungi. No doubt the Potters knew the Drummond Hays, who then lived at Dunkeld. Indeed it is very interesting that Beatrix's paintings in Perth Museum and Art Gallery were found by Mary Noble and Michael Taylor in a portfolio of paintings by Constance Drummond Hay, who was possibly the daughter or niece of this same Francis Drummond Hay. There is another portfolio of paintings by Constance now lodged in the Library of the Royal Botanic Garden Edinburgh. So fungi were a continuing interest in that family! We do know that Francis Drummond Hay brought a specimen of 'The Orange Peel fungus', *Aleuria aurantia*, to Beatrix from the Woods of Strathallan, which she duly painted and recorded with the date 'Oct. 1893' (Hobbs & Whalley, 1985).

The collaboration which had started between McIntosh and Beatrix in Birnam in 1892 continued at least until 1897; we do not know whether further letters were sent between them and there is no indication that she attended his funeral. In Coates (1923) Beatrix is simply referred to as 'a gentlewoman'.

In her letter to McIntosh dated 22 February 1897 Beatrix writes that she has looked at the germinating spores of forty to fifty different species of fungi (Noble, 1987). These were often depicted in line-drawings or colour washes, and sixteen are in the Victoria and Albert Museum, with others in the Armitt Collection at Ambleside. Of all the species she had illustrated, she chose only one, *Flammulina velutipes*, to be the subject of her paper submitted to the Linnean Society of London. *Flammulina* had been illustrated in November 1892 and again in November 1893, growing on gorse, *Ulex*, a very common host of this fungus, although *Flammulina* can be found on a whole range of woody substrates. Beatrix illustrated specimens sent from McIntosh which she left in the airing cupboard, and on opening the tin some days later found etiolated pallid fruiting bodies; she did not recognise them; 'and now another species of fungus has sprung up'. She would not have known that this is the way the same fungus has been grown for food in S.E. Asia for generations, and sold under the name of 'Enoki'. It is only very recently that this fungus has been made available in our own supermarkets

74

and under the same name!

The events leading up to the presentation of her paper on the spore germination of this fungus have been discussed at length (Noble, in Jay [etc.], 1992). Suffice it here to record the relevant dates:

19 May 1896. Beatrix first visited Kew with her uncle Sir Henry Roscoe to see the Director, W.T.Thiselton-Dyer, and George Massee, the mycologist - letter in Kew.

13 June 1896. She visited Kew again to see George Massee.

7 December 1896. She returned to Kew to see Thiselton-Dyer, who was not pleased by the meeting. Thiselton-Dyer later sent a letter to Henry Roscoe, pointing out his niece's indiscretions (Director's file: pers. comm. D.Pegler).

25-26 December 1896. She worked on her paper and it was edited by her uncle. In her *Journal* she writes, 'It will want a great deal more work in references and putting together, but no matter'.

Early January 1897. She saw Massee at Kew, for the fourth time.

31 January 1897. Her *Journal* ends!

1 April 1897. A paper On the Germination of the Spores of the Agaricineae by Miss Helen B. Potter was read at the Linnean Society of London by George Massee.

Later that same day Massee reported on the meeting. Beatrix wrote to McIntosh in September 1897 indicating that her paper had been 'well received, according to Mr Massee, but they say it requires more work in it before it is printed'. As I have previously explained (Watling, 1999), it is not uncommon for papers submitted to scientific journals to be reviewed and returned for additional work, either to the scientific content or for modifications to the text. It could have been the latter, as Beatrix certainly wrote in a very different way from that usually accepted in the scientific community. I know from personal experience that she would have been disappointed under such circumstances. We do not know whether the paper was read purely by title and the illustrations exhibited or if the paper was read in full and returned for modification. Searches at the Linnean Society have not so far unearthed it; Beatrix may even have destroyed it (Jay [etc.], 1992). It was the previous meetings at Kew that probably had some bearing on the decision, as Thiselton-Dyer was the main speaker when Beatrix's presentation was made, and he certainly did not want anyone to distract the audience from his own paper! Beatrix described him as a 'short-tempered, clever man with a very good opinion of his Establishment, and jealous of outsiders', and I can only agree that he was an intimidating character, for more than one other example can be given of similar treatment to male colleagues.

Beatrix's thoughts on their first meeting were not only accurate but discerning. In my opinion this episode did not put her off mycology, as some would lead us to believe, for after April 1897 she was still in correspondence with McIntosh and she was still illustrating fungi. After this date at least sixty-seven paintings, to our knowledge, were prepared, some even as late as 1901, for example *Cystoderma terrei* (=*C. carcharias*), a rather uncommon agaric. She also had an eye for the rarity; thus *Lactarius representaneus*, incorrectly identified as *L. scrobiculatus* was figured from the Lake District in 1900. It is a feature of the Scottish Caledonian forests and only very infrequently found south of the Borders. These observations are hardly those of a person giving up mycology. The Linnean Society meeting came at a time when her Christmas card designs were starting to take off, and her main preoccupation was to become financially independent of her family.

George Massee, who had conveyed the report of the Linnean Society, was a rebellious, rather eccentric, Yorkshire mycologist (Watling, 1982), who had replaced M.C. Cooke, who had himself been unceremoniously dismissed by Thiselton-Dyer – yes, the very same Thiselton-Dyer! Massee had been a little doubtful about Beatrix's results, but had come to appreciate her painstaking work since she often timed the progress of her germinating spores every ten or twenty minutes. Beatrix described Massee as 'a kind, pleasant gentleman. I believe it is rather the fashion to make fun of him, but I can only remark that it is much more interesting to talk to a person with ideas, even if they are not founded on very sufficient evidence'. This is very discerning because Massee continued to be known for his hasty, impatient studies, tinged with a real feel for the organisms. Beatrix liked him because of his unconventional approach compared with others in the scientific community, especially his colleagues at Kew and those at the British Museum (Natural History), which she also visited, asking rather searching questions. Several of the questions were concerned with lichens, in which Beatrix had taken an interest in 1896, and had considered that they might be dual organisms, something which was not current thought in Britain at the time. She successfully germinated the spores of lichens and showed their fungal characteristics. Also, probably by fortuitously linking the germination of some agaric spores and their resulting vegetative stages, and the fact that her cultures were often contaminated with air-borne microfungi, she mused on the idea that larger fungi often have a stage which is mould-like. This again was not accepted as common knowledge in Britain at the time, although the father of German mycology, O. Brefeld, had illustrated some of these structures. However, it took another seventy-five years for the full extent of Beatrix's thoughts to be put into context (Kendrick & Watling, 1979). In addition, Beatrix carefully and accurately monitored the growth of fungi once their spores had germinated, including the anastomosing hyphae found in *Stereum hirsutum* (Jay [etc.] 1992). Again the biological significance of this was not appreciated at the turn of the century but was demonstrated in the work by Ainsworth as a follow-up study to that on the similar *Phanerochaete velutina* (Ainsworth & Rayner, 1986).

Judging from later letters to McIntosh and those deposited at Kew, Beatrix got to know Massee quite well. Realising her undoubted talent, he was keen to persuade her to illustrate discomycetes, a group of tiny cup fungi much less documented than the mushrooms and toadstools, which were being studied by many in continental Europe. Beatrix took the idea to heart, and one can see that by the end of 1896 she had a feel for this group of organisms after illustrating eighteen species and their germinating spores. Other illustrations followed the next summer. These are beautifully and accurately executed and challenge many monographic treatments today. Also in her letters deposited at Kew, she 'continually pays tribute to Kew, repeatedly referring to having got specimens named at Kew or mentions that she will be able to get this and that named at Kew' (Reid, pers. comm.). This points again to the main malevolent character in the whole saga as being Thiselton-Dyer.

The stories of *Aleurodiscus* and *Lachnellula* have been told before (Watling, 1999), but it is interesting to note that on the back of the illustration of the former is pencilled the word 'lichen'. It was at this time that Beatrix was becoming very interested in lichens; did she think that the *Aleurodiscus* was a dual organism? If not, why did she specifically ask for this rather little-known fungus with a restricted distribution and substrate preference? She had certainly described, in her letter to McIntosh, the right characters, including the softening of the old fruiting bodies. She did not realise that the jelly-like structures belonged to another parasitic fungus (Noble & Watling, 1986). It was identified as British only as recently as 1992, but her painting of ninety-five years earlier represents in fact the first record for the British Isles. The fruit-bodies depicted at natural size and their microscopic features are illustrated along with the features of the *Aleurodiscus amorphus* (=*Corticium*) on which it grows. Indeed this fungus *Tremella simplex* was not formally recognised until forty-three years later and then by Jackson & Martin (1940), based on North American collections. The *Aleurodiscus* was not found at Eastwood as some have suspected, but near Inver, growing on its preferred host *Abies alba*.

The *Lachnellula* was one of the discomycetes which she illustrated, and the same plate shows the field differences which separate the parasitic *L. wilkommii*, which grows on swollen lesions on larch trees, and the saprotrophic *L. occidentalis* which grows on woody trash. McIntosh had published on the larch die-back,

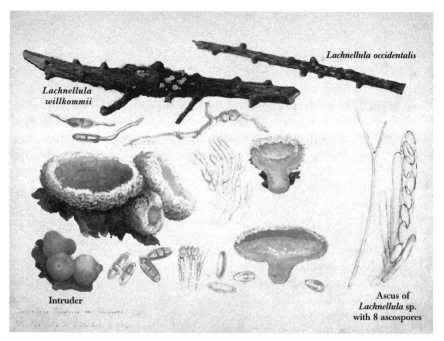

A sheet of paintings which shows several fungi, including *Lachnellula wilkommii*,
L. occidentalis and, an 'intruder', *Nectria*

and with him she discussed in a letter dated 22 January 1897 the differences
based on Lake District, Scottish and Gloucester material, and hypothesised
about the part played by aphids in the disease. Incidentally, on the same plate
as the *Lachnellula* is a small orange, microscopic flask-fungus, pyrenomycete.
Because the spores and structure are so well portrayed it can be identified as
Nectria curcurbitaria which grows on larch; perhaps Beatrix thought that it was an
unopened apothecium of the cup fungus, a trap into which several eminent
mycologists, in parallel circumstances, have also fallen. At this period Beatrix
had followed her father into photography, and there are two mushroom
portraits in the Victoria and Albert Museum of 'Dryad's Saddle', *Polyporus
squamosus*, accompanied by photographs by Rupert Potter.

One of Beatrix's other interests was geology, and on one occasion she dis-
cussed with Massee the characteristics and possible interpretation of a series of
fossils then recently found by Dawson in the Laurentian period and which
Massee believed were the earliest fungi. H.B.Woodward, who was Keeper of
Geology at the British Museum in 1895, showed the suspect fossils to Beatrix.
Alas, we will never know her thoughts on the matter, except that she considered
Massee's statement on the subject 'rather odd, that fungi went back to the

Laurentian'. Over fifty years later it was considered that they were not fungi, but artifacts of sedimentation (Gardiner, 1999). However, fungi do in fact go back a very long way into geological history as fossilised filaments, spores, and simple structures.

Other letters to McIntosh show that by the time the Potters were holidaying at Lennel, near Coldstream in the Scottish Borders, Beatrix had been thinking about the possibility of hybrids in larger fungi, something which perhaps had not occurred to mycologists of her day. Undoubtedly this was instigated by her finding so many different types of bolete which differed very little one from the other. This had concerned her even when she was writing *A Walk with the Funguses*, as indicated earlier. Thus the 'Brown Rough-stalk', *Leccinum scabrum* was figured, and also a collection which can only be the very closely related, *L. melaneum*, with which it is often synonymised by some authors. Modern molecular techniques have confirmed that many of the species in *Leccinum* that she recognised are distinct entities. Another *Leccinum*, the 'Orange Rough-stalk', *L. aurantiacum*, which had been eliminated from the *New Check List of British Agarics and Boleti* (Dennis [etc.], 1960), had in fact been illustrated by Beatrix in 1896 from the Ferry Hotel, and the painting shows its characteristic white then darkening stem-scabrosities and reddish-orange cap. Also the bolete *Boletus porosporus*, which I helped to introduce to science, was figured from Eastwood eighty years before it was validated and it still grows there.

Whilst mentioning molecular studies, one should report that the 'Scaly Tooth', *Sarcodon imbricatum* (=*Hydnum*), illustrated by Beatrix from a specimen collected at Murthley, is of interest. There is exhaustive discussion at the moment as to whether the Scottish material is truly *S. imbricatum* and not the closely related *S. squamosus*, which grows in Scandinavia under pine. The Murthley picture appears to depict a slightly different fungus from that found in the Caledonian forests of Speyside. Further studies are continuing, as McIntosh's material from Murthley is preserved in the Perth Museum.

Another noteworthy fungus pictured by Beatrix is *Amanita crocea*, a yellow orange, typically northern, fungus, probably not well known south of the Border. Although the illustration in the Victoria and Albert Museum has been annotated '*A. fulva*', perhaps during the preparation of Warne's *Wayside and Woodland* book, Beatrix has named this the Northern Grisette. The later annotation on the illustration is wrong. Beatrix was right – it is a distinct species.

Many of Potter's illustrations are upside down, and I thought at first that this was an error. But I am gradually learning of her perception, and am now sure that her real purpose in using this elevation was to show the important charac-

Crepidotus mollis, painted by Beatrix in 1895

ters of the undersurface. The 'Jew's Ear fungus', *Auricularia judae*, is depicted this way as is *Crepidotus* and *Plicaturopsis crispa*, probably from Inver (1892), although I think that *Crepidotus mollis* and *Gloeophyllum sepiarium* (figs. 68 and 194) are incorrectly positioned in *A Victorian Naturalist*. The painting of *Trametes versicolor* (=*Coriolus*) based on material collected in Dunkeld in 1893 is an excellent example of both the upper and the lower surfaces of a fungus.

Many of Beatrix's fungi paintings were first published in *A Victorian Naturalist* in 1992. Some of the captions now need to be modified, as further study in the past few years has led to clarification of the naming of the fungi. For example, fig. 62 shows *Collybia peronata* (=*Gymnopus*) not *C. dryophila*, and in fig. 72 the fungus at the top is a *Mycena* species, not *Agaricus campanellus*, and the one at the bottom is a *Galerina* species. Both the latter are in genera where microscopic examination is required before a definitive identification can be made.

It was a shame that no one told Beatrix how important it is to describe and measure the spores when identifying mushrooms and toadstools, something routine at the present time – after all, she was doing this for the micro-fungi. Most mycologists at that time, however, thought that as the mushrooms were

80

big, they did not need microscopic attention! Had Beatrix drawn the spores at the same time as the fungi, identification would have proved much easier. Many of the fungi in Beatrix's illustrations have yet to be identified definitively, but this must wait for another occasion, and after further scrutiny of the original paintings, perhaps during the next twenty years of the Beatrix Potter Society! I am sure that they will ultimately be identified, since Beatrix was such a good draughtswoman, but some may have to wait until the fungi are found in the fresh state again.

REFERENCES

Ainsworth, A.M. & A.D.M. Rayner, 'Responses of living hyphae with self- and non-self fusions in the basidiomycetes *Phanerochaete velutina*', in *Journal of General Microbiology*, 132: 191-201, 1986

Battrick, E., *Beatrix Potter: The Unknown Years*, Ambleside, Armitt Library & Museum Centre & London, F. Warne, 1999

Coates, H., *A Perthshire Naturalist: Charles MacIntosh of Inver*, London, Fisher Unwin, 1923

Dennis, R.W.G., P.D. Orton, and F.B. Hora, 'The New Check List of British Agarics and Boleti', in *Transactions of the British Mycological Society*, 43, Suppl., 1960

Gardiner, B.G., 'Beatrix Potter's fossils and her interest in geology', in *The Linnean*, 16: 31-46, 1999

Hobbs, A.S., *Beatrix Potter's Art*, London, F. Warne, 1989

Hobbs, A.S. and J.I. Whalley, *Beatrix Potter: The V&A Collection*, London, V&A Museum and F. Warne, 1985

Jackson, H.S. and G.W. Martin, '*Tremella simplex*', in *Mycologia*, 32: 687, 1940

Jay, E., M. Noble and A.S. Hobbs, *A Victorian Naturalist*, London, F. Warne, 1992

Kendrick, W.B. and R. Watling, 'Mitospores in Basidiomycetes', in *The Whole Fungus* 2 (ed. W.B.Kendrick), pp 473-545, Ottawa, National Museums of Canada, 1979

Noble, M., 'The Cryptogamic Society of Scotland 1875-1935-1975', in *Transactions of the Botanical Society of Edinburgh* 42 (Suppl.): 2-27, 1975

Noble, M. 'Beatrix Potter, Naturalist and Mycologist and Charles McIntosh, the Perthshire Naturalist', in *Notes from the Royal Botanic Garden, Edinburgh*, 44: 607-627, 1987

Noble, M. and R. Watling, 'Cup fungi - or Basidiomycetes, and Potterism', in *Bulletin of the British Mycological Society*, 20: 145-147, 1986

Stevenson, J., *British Fungi: Hymenomycetes*, Edinburgh & London, Blackwood & Sons, 1886

Taylor, J., J.I. Whalley, A.S. Hobbs and E. Battrick, *Beatrix Potter 1866-1943: The Artist and Her World*, London, The National Trust & F. Warne, 1987

Watling, R., 'The British Mycological Society: the Yorkshire connection', in *The Naturalist*, 107: 121-129, 1982

'British Mycologists: J. Stevenson, 1836-1903' in *The Mycologist*, 3:45, 1989

'Helen Beatrix Potter', in *The Linnean*, 16: 24-31, 1999

Pleasant visits: Beatrix Potter and Americans

JANE CROWELL MORSE

'MOST WELCOME! I always tell nice Americans to send other nice Americans along. Perhaps "understanding Americans" would be a better adjective than "nice". You come because you understand the books, and love the same old tales that I do – not from any impertinent curiosity.' Seventy years later, Beatrix Potter's 30 April 1930 letter to Helen Dean Fish, editor of children's books for J. P. Lippincott Company, still rings true.

During the twenty years since the founding of the Beatrix Potter Society, exhibitions, publications, lectures, story-telling and conferences have multiplied. In America, the first exhibition at the Pierpont Morgan Library, New York, in May 1988 was followed by 'The World of Peter Rabbit', first shown in Philadelphia at the Museum of Natural History in 1992 and then across the country to California, the state of Washington, and back to Indiana and North Carolina. The exhibitions, and the conferences held in conjunction with them, brought new discoveries and enjoyment to American audiences.

Before the Pierpont Morgan exhibition, it had always been assumed that 1921 was the date that marked the first American visitor to Sawrey, when Anne Carroll Moore, Superintendent of

Beatrix Potter in the doorway at Hill Top: this photograph, previously dated 1907, is now known to have been taken by Charles G. Y. King in 1913

82

Beatrix Potter and her ducklings,
photographed in 1913

Children's Work at the New York Public Library, went there. However, after the exhibition, in response to an article, 'A tale of some tales, and the story of their sly creator', by Timothy Foote, published in the January 1989 issue of the *Smithsonian*, Kenneth Hecht of Wilmette, Illinois, and Helen Lillie of Washington, DC, both wrote letters to the editor, which appeared in the March 1989 *Smithsonian*. Kenneth Hecht's letter adds new information about the importance of the year 1913, when Mr Hecht's grandfather visited Beatrix Potter in May, only five months before her marriage to William Heelis in October.

Kenneth Hecht's letter is as follows:

Dear Sir: For many years every article I have seen about Beatrix Potter has been illustrated by the same photograph of her standing in the doorway of her house, always dated 1907 or, as in the inset on page 81 of your article, 1905. Actually, the picture was taken by my maternal grandfather, Charles G. Y. King in 1913; in his album it is labeled 'Miss Beatrix Potter at Hill Top Farm'.

Here is Grandfather's snapshot from which your detail was taken, showing a winsome Miss Potter outside her vine-festooned farmhouse at Sawrey.

Miss Potter wrote, in a letter to him dated May 27, 1913: 'The photographs have come out remarkably well, your lens must be a very good one . . . . The animals have come out very good – so have some of myself. I am wondering if I am really quite so fat as the stout female with my very small ducklings appears to be . . . .. I wish the house had not been in such an upset condition – any way

83

you will be able to tell your grandchildren that you have seen where Tom Kitten lived, it will make the books still more real to them.

I wrote to Kenneth Hecht and I received from him two letters written to Charles G. Y. King and nine of the photographs he took. Beatrix liked the photographs and requested three each of numbers 3, 5, 6, and 8. The third one is the Hill Top doorway portrait; the fifth another familiar pose with her favorite collie, Kep; the sixth, a portrait of Beatrix Potter with an older gentleman; and the eighth, Beatrix Potter with the ducklings, about which she commented, 'I am much amused with 6 little ducklings, waddling about the garden'.

Although the photographs and the correspondence with Charles G. Y. King have been the most exciting discoveries in response to the exhibition at the Pierpont Morgan Library, additional letters and drawings have been discovered and examined. These have reaffirmed the opinion that Beatrix Potter was a careful observer who drew with meticulous accuracy, that she wanted her drawings to be 'just right', and that she made many variations of a single sketch.

The second letter to the editor of the *Smithsonian* describes a chance encounter when Helen Lillie and her parents visited Sawrey. Helen Lillie wrote:

Dear Sir: Timothy Foote's January article on Beatrix Potter revived for me the most significant day of my life – the day I met her! So young I couldn't even read her books without help, I was on holiday in the Lake District with my Scottish parents. One sunny afternoon we drove up to Sawrey along roads familiar to me from the travels of Peter Rabbit and Pigling Bland. We drew up in front of her house, but we would never have been so pushy as to call on her; we respected privacy.

So my father was enormously embarrassed when, as he balanced me on his shoulders to see over the wall, a large lady in comfortable tweeds came out of the house, a basket over one arm. Hastily he dumped me down, but my mother asked her politely, 'Are you Miss Potter?' 'Yes' said the lady, smiling, 'I am'. All her biographers claim she was so shy she repelled strangers, but that didn't happen to us. She held out her hand to me and asked me my name. Breathlessly, I told her and said I loved her books.

Finding his voice, my father explained he and my mother were interested in her garden. 'Then come in and see it!' she said, and we did. She showed them her best plants, then turned to me again. 'Would you like an egg, Helen, that Sally Henny-Penny laid this morning?' Would I! She took a brown egg from her basket and explained to me carefully how I could 'blow' it so that it would 'keep'. It was a treasured possession until, inevitably, it rolled off the shelf and shattered.

We offered her a lift down to the village, but she said she'd rather walk. Then she shook my hand again, as if I were grown-up, and we went our respective ways.

That afternoon decided the direction my life would take. I was going to be a writer, and I'm glad to say I've seen my name in print many times. But my mental picture of what a writer should look like has always been a big lady in rump-sprung tweeds, the Margaret Rutherford type. She has a lovely open face, a countrywoman's complexion, and wisps of white hair escaping from under her soft, shapeless brown hat. Beatrix Potter.

Although Helen Lillie is a Scot, now and for some years she has been the Washington correspondent of *The Glasgow Herald*. Her chance meeting with Beatrix Potter, a meeting which shaped her career, helps to dispel the conventional belief that Beatrix Potter disliked children.

With reference to Beatrix's desire to have her drawings 'just right', two watercolor drawings from *The Rabbits' Christmas Party* series which were given to Henry P. Coolidge show pencilled-in enlargements of the rabbit's paws. When Beatrix Potter and Henry P. were looking at the pictures, she realized that she had mistakenly given the rabbits the feet of mice. She picked up a pencil and immediately corrected her error. Other examples include a sketch of 'Peter Rabbit's dream of a comfortable bed' in the Westbury Long Island Library and three autographed drawings for the Windermere Fund drawn especially for Mrs. Marion Perry ('I've taken special pains with yours because you wrote me such a nice letter', 30 November 1927). These three are in the Beatrix Potter Collection of The Free Library of Philadelphia.

The first American conference held at The Free Library of Philadelphia in 1992 in conjunction with 'The World of Peter Rabbit' exhibition gave Members the opportunity to see the original manuscript of *The Tailor of Gloucester* with its twelve illustrations, and the privately bound English edition of *The Fairy Caravan* with a note in pencil that reads 'your children [the children of the American publisher, Alexander McKay] may like some "explains" about the pictures'. There are scores of her explanations, not only of her illustrations but also of words and phrases in the text. Among the wonderful illustrations in the Philadelphia collection is a watercolor of a parrot, seen by Beatrix Potter at the home of her former governess, Mrs Moore. These were special discoveries for American Members. In addition, two letters in the Denver, Colorado, Public Library were shared by Betsy Bray and Judy Taylor. One, 19 November 1930, is a book-list of girlhood favorite stories, asking Beatrix Potter to check the ones she had read. The second, 12 July 1936, is to the children in Denver:

Dear Children Friends in Denver,
What can I say to you so far away? I can send my love, and thank you for still remembering Peter Rabbit. It was written more than 40 years ago for a little lame boy. Last week a middle aged active man, a clergyman in Kent, was passing through this Lake country on a motor tour to Scotland. He called here, and

said 'You will not remember me?' I said 'I seem to remember your face'; and it was Noël who had the Peter picture and story first of all in a picture letter! I think that story was good because I wrote it for a real little boy.

I cannot think of more tales to write. There is no sense in going on writing stories when I have nothing more to say. So I will just tell you a true account of my sheep dogs; and you may be interested, because I remember when I was very little I used to love a talk about a colley called 'Sirzah' – how he went out by himself at night and saved a flock of sheep. I have a dog called 'Matt'; his mother is my favorite colley 'Lassie', a very pretty black and white colley. Matt is an ugly dog; but very wise. Last winter was terrible for snow and gales of wind. We had many sheep covered by drifted snow – 'snowed over' as the shepherds say. Matt saved nearly 50. He seems able to smell a sheep buried underneath a 6 foot drift, and he will not leave it. He scratches the snow and barks until help comes, when he assists to dig it out. And in summer he is just as clever, finding sick sheep. Such a dog is worth his weight in gold.

A friend of mine owes his life to his sheep dog. He is a farmer, and he was in the hay loft, cutting out hay from the hay mow (the hay stack) inside the loft. He had carelessly cut too far underneath, and the whole heap of hay toppled over on him. He tried to call help, but he was suffocating, when his old dog heard him and came and dug frantically. And Joe says she had the sense to clear the hay off his face so that he could shout! Indeed I would believe any cleverness of a colley.

I grieve to say that bad men sometimes put honest dogs to very bad uses. Which seems to me to be exceedingly mean - setting on an innocent dog to do their dishonest work. The sheep in this country are often feeding on commons – open land without fences, and there is a lot of sheep stealing. The thieves have a clever quiet dog that does not bark; they carry it with them in a motor van, and when they see a fat sheep near the road in a quiet spot, they stop and the dog catches it for the thief.

Occasionally there are bad dogs who take to sheep stealing, or worrying, on their own account. They are so sly that it is most difficult to detect the culprit. They do not kill their own master's sheep, but go for miles away. And if there is any blood about them they will wash themselves in a river. I once saw a dog that had been in mischief, washing himself. He was rolling in a pool, and ducking his head under.

But it is a rare case. As a rule the sheep dogs are most faithful.

Now I wish you all 'Happy Returns' of your birthdays when the days come round, and I remain your affectionate friend   Beatrix Potter

A second Philadelphia conference in November 1999, again superbly organized by Betsy Bray and Karen Lightner, brought new Members of the Society together to see more of The Free Library's rich and extensive collection and hear lectures. Kara Sewall told us about her own collection and the history of *The Pottergram,* her semi-annual publication that reports on the best and most recent collectibles. Mary Fry described her love of Beatrix Potter and the way

My favourite colley, now growing old.

One of the pages of 'Explains' which Beatrix annotated in the
McKay children's copy of *The Fairy Caravan*

in which it has shaped the success of Rose Tree Cottage, her tea shop and
business in California.

Even before 'The World of Peter Rabbit' toured cities throughout America,
American Members of the Society corresponded, and small groups met inde-
pendently. The Potter-Philes in Indiana have an illustrated newsletter, superbly
edited by Linda Long. Teachers and librarians also bring the tales to life,

appearing before children's groups to tell the stories in the character of Beatrix Potter or as a character in one of the little books. Appreciation of Beatrix Potter as artist and storyteller continues to flourish in America, and yet another generation has come to love *The Tale of Peter Rabbit*, and all the tales.

Beatrix Potter's thoughtful appraisal of Americans is clearly expressed in letters written to Mrs J. Templeman Coolidge on 15 and 30 September 1927:

> I am always pleased to see Americans, I don't know what I think about you as a nation (with a big N!) but the individuals who have looked for Peter Rabbit have all been delightful . . ..
>
> They appreciate the memories of old times, the simple country pleasures, – the homely beauty of the old farm house, the sublime beauty of the silent lonely hills – and – blessed folk – you are not afraid of being laughed at for sentimental.

It all started at Wray

CHRISTOPHER HANSON-SMITH

I T WAS IN 1882, in a small Lake District village called Wray, that the Potter family's association with the Lake District began and where the seeds of Beatrix Potter's connection with the Lake District were sown. That year Rupert Potter was forced to find another property to rent for their annual late-summer holiday, as Dalguise, the small estate on the banks of the River Tay near Dunkeld in Scotland, was for the first time in ten years unavailable owing to a change in ownership. Rupert Potter therefore decided to rent Wray Castle, four miles south of Ambleside, an imposing mock-Norman building overlooking Windermere, which was built in 1840.

Wray Castle has always been a 'white elephant' and it was eventually given to the National Trust in 1929 by an ex-Lord Mayor of Manchester, with the injunction that the Trust could do what it liked with the Castle as long as the thirty-four hectares of wooded land surrounding it were declared inalienable. For many years now a private company has used the Castle for training radio operators for the merchant marine.

The neighbouring church of St. Margaret's had been built at the same time as Wray Castle, whose owner had the right to appoint an incumbent. In 1878 the then owner invited his cousin, a young priest called

Watercolour of the Library at Wray Castle, painted when Beatrix was seventeen

89

Hardwicke Rawnsley, to move to Wray, bringing with him his new bride, Edith Fletcher, whose family lived in Ambleside. The Rawnsleys settled into Wray vicarage and by 1882, when the Potters arrived at Wray Castle, Rawnsley was already campaigning to preserve the natural beauty of the Lake District. He was one of the founders of the Lake District Defence Society whose original committee included such influential figures as Lord Tennyson, then Poet Laureate, Robert Browning and John Ruskin.

The Potters would have soon met the Rawnsleys, and Hardwicke was immediately intrigued by Rupert's interest in collecting autographs of the Lake poets. He also met the Potters' shy daughter who spent so much time absorbed in painting and drawing everything from the richly decorated interiors of the Castle to the many colourful fungi growing in the woods. His wife, Edith, was an accomplished artist - some of her watercolours of Welsh scenery survive - and they both were impressed by Beatrix's obvious talent.

The Potters never returned to Wray Castle, but between 1885 and 1907 the Lake District became their favourite choice for late summer holidays. Beatrix herself was already drawn to the idyllic countryside around Esthwaite Water, a few miles west of Wray, and she had been delighted when her father took a house in Near Sawrey in 1896, with a wonderful view up the lake towards Hawkshead. It was then called Lakefield, but today it is a guesthouse with the Old Norse name of Ees Wyke. Other places rented by the Potters were Lingholm and Fawe Park, both substantial houses on the west shore of Derwentwater.

When the Potters stayed at Lakefield their coachman and his family were accommodated at nearby Hill Top farm, so it was a place already known to Beatrix when the royalties from the publication of her first little books, together with a small legacy, enabled her to buy it in 1905. The purchase of this working fell farm added a new dimension to Beatrix's life. She recalled her earlier conversations with Rawnsley and remembered his passionate desire to preserve the Lake District. While she was well aware of the need to counter unsuitable development, unlike Rawnsley she realised that, in this man-made environment, the traditional way of life of the farmers and the country folk also had to be protected.

With Hill Top farm had come a flock of Herdwicks, together with the less hardy Swaledale or Scots Blackface breeds which are well suited for crossing with other lowland sheep. The custom in the Lake District is for the sheep to belong to the farm, so that when a farm changes hands the incoming owner or tenant takes over all the sheep as well. Likewise when he (or she) leaves the farm he has to hand over the same number of sheep with which he started. Thus

Photograph of Mrs William Heelis (Beatrix Potter) judging sheep at
Keswick in the late 1930s

today the National Trust, which owns about seventy fell farms, also owns
approximately 30,000 Herdwick sheep which are managed by its tenants.

In 1924 Beatrix Potter, now married to William Heelis, was rich enough to
buy Troutbeck Park farm, east of Windermere. It was her largest acquisition to
date - 1800 acres of wonderful fell country, and to run it she lured the shepherd
Tom Storey away from a neighbouring farmer by offering him more money.
Thus began a partnership, which, in the early 1930s, resulted in Mrs Heelis's
Herdwick ewes winning all the trophies at the various local agricultural shows.
Tom's son, Geoffrey, grew up in the same mould and was later to become the
tenant of Hill Top farm, where to this day the 'smit' or identifying mark on the
fleece of every sheep is a large 'H' for Heelis.

Whereas Beatrix had been steadily buying up vacant farms and farm buildings, in order to stop them falling into the hands of 'offcomers' who usually had
no interest in keeping the land linked to the buildings, Rawnsley's idea had been
to ensure that open land did not become private and enclosed, thereby keeping
out the public. Rawnsley was successful in whipping up national public support
for a local campaign to prevent the closure of footpaths by the landowners on
the lower flanks of Skiddaw, up behind Keswick, and on Catbells, a prominent
fell overlooking the western shore of Derwentwater – and the footpaths
remained open. Rupert Potter became one of the National Trust's first Life
Members, and the whole Potter family would have been aware of Rawnsley's
activities.

In 1901 Beatrix was staying at Lingholm and was making sketches of the Derwentwater scenery in preparation for her story about Squirrel Nutkin. She knew well the stretch of lakeshore called Brandelhow which the fledgling National Trust was seeking to buy by public appeal. The following year the 100 acres were successfully bought by the Trust and for the first time the public had full access. Using money raised by public appeals, the Trust went on to acquire a succession of open spaces in the Lake District, including Aira Force and Gowbarrow on Ullswater in 1906, with the future President of the United

Beatrix with Canon Hardwicke Rawnsley and his son Noel in the gardens at Lingholm; photograph taken by Rupert Potter in 1885 or 1887

States, Woodrow Wilson, present at the opening ceremony. To all these public appeals the Potter family might well have contributed and, after her father's death in 1913, Beatrix continued to support the Trust. She always insisted that her contributions were to be anonymous and, when the Trust bought Queen Adelaide's Hill on Windermere in 1913, she wrote to Rawnsley to explain that she would send him more money when she was paid for a pig she had recently sold.

In 1930 Beatrix became even more closely associated with the Trust when the Monk Coniston estate of 4,000 acres was put up for sale. The land included a farm on the Tilberthwaite fells, Holme Ground, which one of the paternal grandparents of Beatrix, the Cromptons, had once owned. There was, therefore, every incentive for Beatrix to help the Trust to buy the estate. Her solution was to put up the money for the purchase herself, so as to secure the land, and then to wait for the repayment of half the amount when the Trust had time to raise it. Meanwhile she offered to manage the farms herself while the Trust searched for a suitable land agent to take them over. Beatrix also promised that when she died her half of the estate would be bequeathed to the Trust, together with all her other farms.

The appointment of a land agent and the hand-over to him of the farms was not without drama. Beatrix at one stage, in 1938 wrote, 'I regret heartily that I ever presented Holme Ground to the Trust . . . he [the new agent, Bruce Thompson] seems to have no understanding about anything and he is not learning either'. And five months later she told the Trust, 'A man cannot help having been born dull. Thompson is supercilious as well'.

The problems over the Monk Coniston estate and the Trust were eventually resolved and, thanks to Beatrix, the Trust was left with a superb tract of the central Lake District, including Tarn Hows, which attracts more visitors than any other site in the fell country. Hardwicke Rawnsley had died in 1920 and sadly did not see how successfully the principles of land acquisition for public enjoyment, which he had first proclaimed, had been so faithfully followed by Beatrix.

In 1966 at an exhibition at the Abbot Hall Gallery in Kendal, to mark the centenary of Beatrix's birth, Conrad Rawnsley, Hardwicke's grandson, gave a moving speech. In it he claimed that had Beatrix still been a spinster in 1916 when Hardwicke's first wife, Edith, died, his grandfather might well have asked Beatrix for her hand in marriage. Whatever one may think of this surmise there is no gainsaying the great affection and mutual respect that had existed between Beatrix and Hardwicke ever since they first met at Wray back in 1882. Without that friendship Beatrix might never have become such a dedicated and generous supporter of the National Trust. And in that case, what might have happened to all those farms and acres of fell which she had collected with such foresight?

We must therefore be profoundly grateful that it DID all begin at Wray . . .

One of the 'off-road' footpaths constructed by the National Trust, to which the Beatrix Potter Society made a financial contribution

93

Restoring the Countryside Legacy

PAUL FARRINGTON

BEFORE I BEGIN, I must put in a disclaimer by saying that the views expressed here will be my own and are from the perspective of a National Trust Countryside Warden, and do not necessarily reflect the official views of the Trust.

My title, 'Restoring the Countryside Legacy', would suggest that if restoration is needed then some deterioration has taken place in those countryside properties left to the Trust's care by Beatrix Potter. It would be more surprising if nothing of the farmland and woodland had changed in the last fifty or sixty years. In fact, the massive increase in the number of people visiting places like Tarn Hows and Hill Top has had a dramatic effect in terms of erosion and loss of vegetation and has also led to more roads and car parks.

Modern intensive farming no longer needs the old machinery,
which rusts away in the corners of fields

As a result of changes in farming practices since the 1940s, the fields and hedgerows, which on the face of it look quite healthy, have suffered greatly in their nature conservation value. Intensive grazing, heavy fertiliser application and extensive drainage, have led to fields which were once rich in wildflowers, insects and birds, becoming very much less diverse and in many cases supporting only a handful of different types of grasses and flowers and a few nesting birds. Hedgerows have been neglected, as farming practices have favoured wire fences and mechanical cutting as opposed to traditional hedgelaying. Woodlands too have been managed with the emphasis on commercial timber production, with new coniferous plantations of spruce and larch being introduced at the expense of the native oak and ash. To be fair, these changes have happened all over Britain, not just on Beatrix Potter's farms, and they have happened for a number of reasons.

The intensification of farming is something that was encouraged during the war years for obvious reasons and the policy was continued in the following decades by subsequent governments and by European grants and subsidies. In its simplest form this meant maximising production and income on farms by keeping the largest possible number of sheep and cattle, and in this the Potter farms were managed no differently from other Lake District farms. At this time too the National Trust in the Lake District was experiencing a rapid growth both in membership and in the ownership of countryside properties. The threat to the countryside in the Lake District, which Beatrix was very much aware of, continued and if anything intensified, so that the need to acquire important properties became a priority. The active management of existing properties, Potter farms included, perhaps took second place as a result of this. In addition, the 'benign' ownership of the Trust, and the mere fact that the land was being used for agricultural purposes, was deemed in itself to be enough to protect them. To be fair to previous NT land agents and other staff, at this time the tenant/landlord relationship was different, and the Trust's ability to influence management was more limited. The result, however, was that in the period between the 1940s and the 1980s we lost some of the diverse and traditional flora and fauna which would have been very familiar to Beatrix Potter: otters, barn owls, corncrakes, great crested newts and fresh-water crayfish, for example. As we lose wild flowers, wetlands, and hedgerows, we also lose the insects and the birds which rely on these for their survival.

I wonder what Beatrix would have said or done about the management on her farms, under these new pressures? It would have taken a courageous, outspoken, and forward looking person, like her, to question what was happening in agriculture at the time, and I think she would have had divided loyalties between protecting the local flora and fauna which she loved, and supporting the local farming community of which she was part.

If the period between 1940 and 1980 was for the Trust about acquisition and growth, then the period since 1980 has been about consolidation. Improving the management of existing properties, including the Beatrix Potter farms, has become the main priority, and balancing the demands of farming with those of nature conservation, access and recreation has been the greatest challenge.

The work that the National Trust Wardens and Estate staff have undertaken in recent years on the Beatrix Potter properties could loosely be gathered under four headings: field boundary repairs, access, woodland management and nature conservation. The traditional types of field boundary which we find in this part of the Lake District form an important element in the character of the area, and require active management. Flagstone fences have been a feature of the Hawkshead and Coniston areas for many centuries, and recently the Trust has undertaken repair work on some of the more high profile sections. The Estate team uses traditional locally quarried stone, traditional hammers and chisels (and possibly a few traditional swear words), as they cut the very heavy and sharp-edged flagstones to size, and manoeuvre them into place. The secret of a successful flagstone boundary repair is to ensure that each flagstone has overlapping edges, which interlock with the neighbouring stones, so that each stone supports those on either side. This type of repair is expensive (around £60 per metre) and time consuming, but hopefully the results will remain for another 200 years.

Over the past twenty years hedge re-instatement has been an important feature of work programmes on the Beatrix Potter farms. The process involves repairing the old 'kest' or hedge bank by building it up with soil and stone, erecting a stockproof fence on either side of the kest, and then planting with a mixture of hawthorn, blackthorn, holly, and hazel, and with occasional oaks, crab apple and bird cherry. When these hedges are established, after about ten years, they are ready for laying. This is undertaken between November and February to minimise the disturbance to wildlife, and involves disentangling the trees and their branches, cutting out the dead wood and trimming back to leave only the straight strong growth. These are then cut four-fifths of the way through at the base, leaving one-fifth of the bark and cambium so that the trees are still alive, and then these 'pleachers' as they are called, are laid over almost horizontally and pegged in place. New growth takes place at the base and along the length of the newly laid tree, and this new growth will be laid in years to come.

Hedge re-instatement is one of those projects which has benefits all round and

Lakeland scenery between Hawkshead and Ambleside, showing some of the dry stone walls of the area

they are a valuable habitat for a whole range of insects, birds and mammals as well as the many traditional hedgerow flowers like honeysuckle, lesser celandine, bluebells and stitchwort. And of course they are an important feature of the landscape in their own right.

There are not as many dry stone walls around Hawkshead as in some areas of the Lake District but we still get involved in repairing gaps, particularly when the damage is caused by visitors. The popularity of the whole area around Hawkshead and Coniston and the high level of access that this involves requires active management, particularly around the 'honeypot' areas like Tarn Hows, Hawkshead Village and Hill Top. There are many miles of off-road footpaths which have been specially constructed to make it safer and more enjoyable for people to get around; one of them, between the Windermere Ferry and Hill Top, was supported by the Beatrix Potter Society and constructed by the National Trust and National Park staff (see page 93). In addition, each year the Trust replaces hundreds of gates, stiles and fingerposts. A section of boardwalk at Moss Eccles Tarn has been constructed recently, also with the financial assistance of the Beatrix Potter Society, and it will help people to gain access around the west side of Moss Eccles, while protecting the tarn-side vegetation, which includes water mint and forget-me-nots.

Work in the woodlands includes safety work, such as removing dangerous branches, etc.; control of invasive, non-native species such as rhododendron,

97

beech and sycamore; promotion of the natural regeneration of oak, ash, holly and hazel; fencing off small woodlands which were previously unfenced in order to encourage natural regeneration; and also planting and putting guards around individual trees.

Nature conservation has always been a consideration when managing our countryside properties, but recently it has become a strong central theme when considering changes in management to our farmland and woodland; it is important that farming practice should not be at the expense of the natural world. The aim of our nature conservation policy is to encourage diversity, in order to create and maintain as wide a range of habitats as possible. The Trust will, wherever possible, involve its farm tenants in the decision-making process and ensure that they gain some benefit, either financial or otherwise, from the measures that we introduce. We are helped in this by the Government's Environmentally Sensitive Area Scheme (ESA), by which means our tenants can get payments for farming in an environmentally sensitive way. At Hill Top farm we have been monitoring the hay meadows for the past four years, to see how the wild flower communities have been changing since the introduction of new, less intensive, management. There have been fewer sheep grazing in the fields, which have been cut later than other fields to allow the wild flowers to set their seed. So far they seem to be doing well, but we continue to monitor them.

Just north of Moss Eccles Tarn we are about to start a juniper regeneration project, with the financial assistance of the Beatrix Potter Society. We are hoping to fence off an area of crag and encourage the juniper tree cover to spread by preparing the ground and planting seedlings. At High Tock How farm a recent change of tenant has enabled us to make some major nature conservation improvements through a new tenancy agreement. We have plans to fence off the edges of Ford Wood Beck, to control the grazing, and to protect and enhance the beck-edge vegetation and tree cover, whilst at the same time improving water quality. This type of project is being carried out on several of the Beatrix Potter farms, and usually the tenants can get increased ESA payments for agreeing to have this work done. We have also put restrictions on fertiliser application and grazing levels on most of the fields surrounding Blelham Tarn, which is a Site of Special Scientific Interest and a National Nature Reserve, the hope being that the water quality will improve and that the remnants of the valuable flower communities, which are largely confined to field edges, will in time spread more widely. We are also encouraging some parts of fields to become flooded by allowing drains to block up, because wet field areas are a very valuable habitat for certain flowers, and insects like the Golden Ringed Dragonfly.

All these measures are typical of the changes in management that are being encouraged across the Beatrix Potter farms, but they are not always easily accepted or welcomed because they are the complete opposite of what was previously considered to be good farming practice. In effect, what the Trust has been trying to achieve over the past twenty years has been to recreate the rural landscape of the 1920s and 1930s, when farming was more in balance with the natural world, and farm practices were more sustainable, less intensive, and allowed a more diverse range of habitats to co-exist. The challenge facing the Trust and its farmers over the next fifty years is how to ensure the sustainable management of its farmland, while still keeping these small individual farm units viable as working farms in a dramatically changing world economy.

Most of you will be aware of the crisis facing farming in Britain today. There is a strong feeling amongst many farmers that farming has changed for ever. This has been brought about by a number of factors: the strength of the pound has meant that exports of beef and lamb have suffered; world markets and food production have changed and there is new and increased competition from other countries; and improved animal welfare and environmental standards have meant that old farm buildings are often no longer appropriate for modern farming practices. Massive investment and new farm buildings are sometimes not practical or justifiable. This situation is not new. When farming in the Lake

Typical of vernacular Lakeland architecture is this picture of Glencoyne Farmhouse and barn, which was one of the farms bequeathed by Beatrix Potter to the National Trust

District was going through a recession in the late 1920s and 1930s, Beatrix Potter was quick to encourage her tenant farmers to diversify, and to find alternative forms of income, by providing accommodation or afternoon teas for visitors. This is what many of our tenants have been doing with the help and encouragement of the Trust. High Loanthwaite and High Tock How farms run bed and breakfast businesses and Tock How also has a holiday cottage. Such activities, which were once sidelines, now often provide as much income as the farming side of the business.

Grants and subsidies have changed dramatically in the past ten years, and have moved away from headage payments which encouraged each farm to maximise the number of sheep and cattle, towards area payments which are based on nature conservation and access principles, often paying farmers to reduce the amount of grazing in certain fields or to fence off woodlands or river banks. Some of the National Trust tenants on the larger farms do very well out of this system, others on smaller farms, who invested money in the late 1980s and early 90s are suffering as their incomes have dropped drastically.

I am sure Beatrix Potter would be very disappointed to see how the markets for Herdwick meat and wool, in particular, have suffered. Wool in general, and particularly the dark tough Herdwick wool, is no longer in demand, as people prefer lighter synthetic fabrics, and such things as wool carpets are out of favour. The Herdwick Sheepbreeders Association in particular has been very active in encouraging selective breeding in order to maintain the genetic integrity of the breed. Also several local farmers, particularly in Langdale, are running a 'fell bred' scheme encouraging local hotels and restaurants to use traditional local Herdwick lamb: selling the meat direct, and cutting out the middle-men. This type of scheme appears to be working quite well and may be important to the future of Herdwick sheep in the Lake District. The National Trust fully supports this work and is also exploring ways of boosting Herdwick products. The Trust recently hosted a launch of Herdwick carpets by the British Wool Marketing Board at Hill Top, something Beatrix Potter herself would have warmly welcomed.

The future of farming looks uncertain, and some of our tenant farmers are struggling. We certainly hope this will be a temporary state of affairs, but the future for the woods, fields, wetlands and becks looks more promising now than it has done for fifty years. This has been typified by the return of breeding barn owls to Tock How farm for the first time in many years, a trend which we hope will be followed by a whole range of other species familiar to Beatrix Potter, such as otters, corncrakes, or crayfish, thus restoring the countryside legacy.

Index

Page numbers in **bold type** refer to illustrations. Since the whole of this volume is devoted to aspects of Beatrix Potter's life and work the only entries under her name in this Index refer to pictures of her.

The Beatrix Potter Society

The Beatrix Potter Society was founded in 1980 by a group of people professionally involved in the curatorship of Beatrix Potter material. It exists to promote the study and appreciation of the life and works of Beatrix Potter (1866-1943), who was not only the author and illustrator of *The Tale of Peter Rabbit* and other classics of children's literature, but also a Natural History artist, diarist, farmer and conservationist - in the latter capacity she was responsible for the preservation of large areas of the Lake District through her gifts to the National Trust.

The Society is a registered charity and its membership is worldwide. Its activities include regular talks and meetings in London and visits to places connected with Beatrix Potter. An annual Linder Memorial Lecture is given each spring to commemorate the contribution made to Beatrix Potter studies by Leslie Linder and his sister Enid. The first of these was given at the Victoria and Albert Museum by Margaret Lane, as Patron of the Society. Biennial Study Conferences are held in the Lake District and Scotland and are attended by Members from around the world.

A quarterly *Newsletter,* issued free to Members, contains articles on a wide range of topics as well as information about meetings and visits, reviews of books and exhibitions, Members' letters, and news of Beatrix Potter collections both in the United Kingdom and elsewhere. The Society also publishes the proceedings of its Study Conferences and other works of original research.

For further information write to: The Beatrix Potter Society Office, Resources for Business, South Park Road, Macclesfield, SKI 1 6SH.